Scapegoats at Work

Scapegoats at Work
Taking the Bull's-Eye Off Your Back

JOHN M. DYCKMAN

AND

JOSEPH A. CUTLER

PRAEGER

Westport, Connecticut
London

Library of Congress Cataloging-in-Publication Data

Dyckman, John M., 1945–
    Scapegoats at work : taking the bull's eye off your back / John M. Dyckman and Joseph
A. Cutler.
      p. cm.
    Includes bibliographical references and index.
    ISBN 0–275–98182–7 (alk. paper)
    1. Organizational behavior. 2. Scapegoat—Psychological aspects. 3. Office politics.
I. Cutler, Joseph A., 1949– II. Title.
    HD58.7.D93 2003
    650.1′3—dc22   2003057975

British Library Cataloguing in Publication Data is available.

Library of Congress Catalog Card Number: 2003057975
ISBN: 0–275–98182–7

First published in 2003

Praeger Publishers, 88 Post Road West, Westport, CT 06881
An imprint of Greenwood Publishing Group, Inc.
www.praeger.com

Printed in the United States of America

The paper used in this book complies with the
Permanent Paper Standard issued by the National
Information Standards Organization (Z39.48–1984).

10 9 8 7 6 5 4 3 2 1

Contents

Acknowledgments

It is traditional—and appropriate—to acknowledge and thank all those who contributed to the creation of a book. We have had help from many sources. We wish to recognize and thank them.

Eric Greenleaf, Susanne Dyckman, Robert Rosenbaum, Roger Spence, Thomas Turman, and Tanya Wilkinson all read versions of the manuscript and offered suggestions and encouragement in approximately equal doses. Additionally, we would like to acknowledge Mary Boyvey, Peter Cutler, Sandi Cutler, Claudia Kruse, and Paul Minsky for their encouragement and input. Our spouses, Diana Sloat and Ellen Schwartz, tolerated the disappointments and delays that too often accompany a project like this. Michael Riera, once a student of John's, became his teacher and put him in touch with Liz Trupin-Pulli. Liz became our agent and helped bring the project from proposal to publication.

Initially Joe came to John with the idea to do this book. We developed the content in the readings and research that we each did and in conversations and meetings that we had weekly for more than a year. Most of the writing fell to John. Joe wrote the opening vignette about Jack and contributed to the checklist in chapter 7. Joe also wrote the vignettes of Fred, Alice, and Roxanne in chapter 11, as well as some brief passages of chapter 11.

The foundations of this book rest on the help of those whom we cannot thank by name—those we have known and attempted to help cope with the pain of scapegoating. Their experiences and courage in exploring how they got there, and what they could do about it, brought the project to life. We have disguised their identities, changed their occupations, ages, even genders, and have sometimes combined individual stories into composites. It is to them that this book is dedicated.

CHAPTER 1

The Costs of Scapegoating

Jack's head was pounding as he crossed the wet parking lot in the afternoon rain. He carried a cardboard box with photos of his family and a few books he'd kept in his office. The security guard watched him, stone-faced, from the curb by the back door. Jack looked up at the office windows. Only one face was visible—that of a coworker who had warned him that this day was coming. The face was expressionless.

Jack was sweating, his heart racing, his face flushed hot with shame and rage. His stomach was in a cold knot. He was filled with disbelief, humiliation, and fear. What was he going to tell his wife? His children? He was at a loss for words. He had been "let go"—fired, terminated. It was Friday afternoon, the classic day and time for these things. He hadn't really seen it coming, though he had feared it. He was stunned and confused when his supervisor called him into his office and fired him. Just like that. Well, almost.

Jack had known things weren't right for months now, but had not been sure of what to do, how to handle it. He had tried to talk with his wife but was too ashamed of the growing feelings of failure at work, and he had gradually stopped telling her how bad it was. He just told her that he was sick of being picked on and was thinking of transferring or looking for another job. She had encouraged him to leave. She believed in him, didn't blame him for everything, as they did at work. But he had let her down. He hadn't looked for another job. Like a deer in the headlights, he had stood in the middle of the road until the truck had hit him. Mostly he blamed himself.

A sudden image of himself jumping off the bridge on his way home filled his mind. It seemed so easy, so quick. He couldn't face his wife, his family. Fired. How would he get another job? He was ruined. They could lose the house. His wife would leave him. His children would look at him with pity and contempt. Teenagers hate weakness, failure. They would hate him. Like he hated himself. As he got into the car, he felt relief. That was it. Off the bridge. Now. He started the car and drove it out of the company parking lot. He could see the security guard in the rearview mirror, waiting for him to be gone. He hated them all. Let his death be on their heads.

As he drove, he thought back over the last few months at work. How his problems had snowballed. With disbelief he had watched small problems mount, felt coworkers talking about him behind his back, blaming him for things over which he had no control. Then they began to avoid him. They were polite. No more than that. Not friendly, not social. Polite. He couldn't break through it. He felt like he'd failed some test. Somehow he'd been chosen, blamed, and then driven out.

He had heard about others in the company who had had this happen, but he had laughed and believed the stories about their weakness, their lack of political skills, their poor timing, and their bad luck. He had felt the relief each time one of them had left. At least the focus was not on him. They had found the problem and taken care of it. Gotten rid of it. With dread he had realized, too late, that he was next. And he felt helpless to stop it. He didn't know how to handle the unfairness of it, or how to fight it. It was too late.

As he drove through the light rain, he got angrier and angrier. As he neared the bridge, he pulled off the side of the road, turned off the motor, and sat, staring through the gray afternoon at the bridge span rising over the dark water a few hundred yards ahead. "Kill myself? Hell no!" he thought. "I'll kill my boss!"

Jack quickly dismissed the angry fantasies as crazy. Rage, mixed with shame, still flooded him. He sat, paralyzed, in the late afternoon drizzle, as wave after wave of emotion and suicidal, then revengeful, images washed through him. Slowly they subsided, leaving him exhausted, sad, and confused. Then a vivid memory of playing with his children came to him. No. He couldn't do that to them. Abandon them. Ruin their lives. No.

He started the car and drove quickly over the bridge, not once looking over the side at the water far below. He did not know what to do, but he was going to survive this. Somehow. As he drove toward his home, he thought about his sister who lived far away. And about his pastor, whom he did not talk to regularly, but who had helped his wife and him get through the death of his wife's father. As he drove, he came to a decision. He would go home. Tell his wife. Call the pastor. Call his sister. He did not know how they could help, but he had no one else. As he pulled up into his driveway, he was cold, sweating, and pale.

His wife did not abandon him though she was upset. She did not blame him, but did ask him if he had done anything he hadn't told her about. Hurt, he denied keeping any secrets. The truth was shameful enough. He told his children that he had quit. They were upset that he didn't have another job first. He shrugged, went upstairs, turned on the TV, and stared into space, drinking beer, silent, late into the night.

The next morning he called the pastor and then his sister, who told him that she had seen a counselor when she had problems at work. The counselor had related the work problems to her childhood. It was expensive and took a long time, but it had helped her a lot.

Jack listened in disbelief. He had gotten the same recommendation from the pastor. Counseling. A shrink. Like it was all his fault. Like he'd been damaged as a child and somehow everyone at work could see it, like a name tag or a limp. He never talked about his childhood to anyone, not even his wife. What she knew she had heard from his sister, after the funeral, over dinner. His wife had looked at him differently from that day on. She was more patient with him, but he felt embarrassed by her sympathy. Now everyone was telling him he needed a shrink. How was a shrink going to change those jerks at work that scapegoated one person after another, year after year? How was a shrink going to protect him from it happening again, on another job, if he ever got one?

Jack knew he felt awful and that he had to do something about it. He asked his pastor for the name of a therapist, and he also asked his family doctor for one. He even looked in the phone book and asked his wife for help in finding one. He couldn't wait. He was too depressed to go on as he was. His family doctor gave him some pills for depression, and after a few weeks they helped him enough to call one of the counselors. He set up an appointment, resentful, ashamed, hoping for a miracle, but doubting that therapy had anything to offer him besides a painful rehash of his childhood.

Jack's story is one that is repeated in the American workplace many thousands of times a year. We know from our experience working with patients who come into our practices with job stress, depression, and anxiety that scapegoating is a common problem in the workplace. Most workers who suffer from it are isolated and blame themselves as their managers and coworkers have blamed them. Sometimes a vague sense that "it is not fair" is their only clue that there may be larger forces at work, institutional forces, workplace culture forces that operate like a powerful undertow on a seemingly quiet beach.

One-quarter of employees rate their jobs as the number one stressor in their lives.[1] Three-quarters believe that the worker has more on-the-job stress now than a generation ago.[2] Health care costs are nearly 50 percent greater for workers who report high levels of job stress.[3] The effects of job stress may appear in forms as mild as low morale, or as pronounced as prolonged absence or turnover due to serious illness. When absenteeism, reduced productivity, employee turnover, as well as direct costs of medical, legal, and insurance fees related to job stress claims are added together, they are estimated to cost U.S. industry a staggering $300 billion annually.[4]

The National Institute for Occupational Safety and Health (NIOSH) evaluates the risk of injury and illness among workers based on a combination of factors, including job conditions, individual employee personality, and situational factors.[5] Some working conditions are inherently stressful (including some management styles characterized by poor communication, exclusion of workers in decision making, etc.), and some workers have fewer coping skills and social support to deal with stress. It generally takes a combination of these factors to result in injury due to "job stress."

In rare but often highly publicized instances, job stress can even lead to workplace violence. Disputes among coworkers and with customers and clients account for about 10 percent of workplace homicides.[6] Persons who feel isolated, marginalized, and ridiculed sometimes resort to violence in a desperate attempt to force others to acknowledge their power and even their existence as individuals.[7] Although no government agency collects statistics on cases in which a company copes with problems by identifying, blaming, isolating, and excluding workers, we are convinced that many of the cases of "job stress" that are reported are instances of this process—the process of scapegoating.

Scapegoating has been around for thousands of years and seems to be built into the human condition. But that doesn't mean that workers can't learn to identify it and subsequently protect themselves. Workplace cultures can be changed, but individual behaviors can be changed more easily. Men like Jack and women like Carla, whom we will also follow as she copes with scapegoating on her nursing job, can learn to identify the way that potential scapegoats are targeted by bosses and coworkers, then are isolated, and finally excluded from the workplace.

The authors of this book met a number of years ago when we both worked in an outpatient clinic for a large health maintenance organization. Being young and idealistic, we were both puzzled by an apparent paradox of our work situation: even though we found most of our colleagues individually to be highly intelligent and personable, we noticed that as a group we functioned much less ably. This was especially surprising since as psychotherapists our business was awareness—of ourselves, of others, and of the group process.

One of the tendencies that seemed especially difficult to understand was the lack of support for different views in administrative meetings—even when individuals had previously privately expressed support for the dissenting viewpoints. The role of the dissenter seemed to be concentrated in one or two staff members. As administration became more impatient with dissent, the dissenter would also become more impatient and insistent, increasingly isolated, and subtly (and sometimes directly) labeled as undesirable. Furthermore, the dissenter appeared to become increasingly identified with that role, that is, he or she began to feel more and more incapable of stepping back from it.

Interestingly, when the dissenters left the organization, different members of the staff gradually stepped into the role of the identified "other" who spoke things that the management team did not want to hear. They then came to be seen as being "out of step," and their opinions were marginalized. These new "recruits" began to feel bitter, impatient, and different. In time they also left, and the pattern repeated again.

A number of years later, Joseph began to study the structure of organizations, and with the distance of time and intervening jobs, he decided that the pattern we had observed years before was part of a larger problem of the organization of the structure of the workplace and of the minds of the workers. He approached me with the idea of this book. Both of us had seen the confusion, pain, and rage that scapegoating produces. We also knew that there are some things that can be done to relieve and prevent this distress.

Jack sat in the therapist's waiting room alternating between feeling self-conscious and furious. He wondered what a therapist could possibly know about the games that bosses and coworkers can play. Would this counselor look down on him? Jack dreaded talking about his family. He especially dreaded admitting "weakness" to a man. His sister had told him that his anger might have to do with their father, who used to beat them mercilessly when he had been drinking.

When the therapist appeared and invited him in, Jack felt filled with shame and humiliation. Still, Jack was determined to do the right thing, so he took a deep breath and said, "I need to know what's wrong with me. You may have to push me hard—I don't want you to let me just blame everyone else."

The therapist waited a minute, then nodded and replied, "Let's see what you need. Perhaps you need to be pushed hard, but maybe you don't. Let's not assume that everyone at your job was blameless, and while we're at it, let's not use the word 'blame' for a while. Let's look at what happened at work, how you got there, and how you can see it coming next time."

Jack felt guilty now for the relief he'd felt when others had been blamed for the problems of the department. He had seen a movie once about how wild hyenas hunted in packs. They circled the herd of gazelles, looking for one that was different—young, old, weak, ill. As they closed in on it, the rest of the herd ran on to safety. He used to be one of the survivors, but now he had been left behind. At work there had been a few who had tried to help, had given him advice. His face still flushed with shame and anger as he recalled the last six months. But he also began to feel the stirrings of a new emotion: he began to feel curious about what had happened.

HOW TO USE THIS BOOK

Our primary concern is to help both workers and managers understand how scapegoating occurs in the workplace, how to recognize it, how to counter it, and, ultimately, how to avoid it entirely. Since we believe that the key to preventing scapegoating is to understand it, we start with a description of the origins of the scapegoat—both in religion and psychology. There is a good deal of scholarly research in related areas, and we have reserved most of the discussion of this for the notes. Readers who are interested in pursuing these topics will find the notes useful; however, we are most interested in helping people understand and avoid scapegoating in their daily lives, and the book can be read with or without the notes.

We have included many case examples from our work with individuals and organizations. In order to protect privacy, we have changed names and identifying details. In some instances we have combined case material to further disguise the parties.

Scapegoating is a complex phenomenon. Thinking in "all or none" terms promotes blaming and makes it harder to reabsorb the contradictions and ambiguities that are the painful but necessary job of taking real personal responsibility. Scapegoated individuals are themselves often caught in an *all or nothing/right or wrong* view of the world. They feel that it is either their entire fault, or all the fault of the other. We have found that the best results come from helping individuals discover and change the ways that they unconsciously participate in the social process of scapegoating. This involves becoming aware of one's own contribution to the problem—what psychotherapists call the "hook of reality" on which others hang distorted attributions called *projections.* That is, there is usually some *real* basis for the exaggerated and negative evaluations that people use to attempt to cope with their own sense that something is wrong.

Unfortunately, social systems often equate being different with being wrong. We believe that consciously recognizing and holding differences between persons can be an important source of creativity. This can benefit both the individual and the organization.

Just as individuals are different, so are organizations. Different acts are necessary in different situations, so there is no one answer that will solve each situation. Consider the examples in each section as possibilities rather than formulae. If you are facing scapegoating personally, you may find it useful to get consultation—from trusted friends, religious advisors, and/or from professionals in organizational development (often found in Employee Assistance programs), psychology, or law.

One of the tasks of truly "growing up" is recognizing that there is no one outside yourself who will come to save you. Salvation, if it can be called that, is a lonely and painful process. We have written this book to encourage and accompany this journey and to indicate that there are many different ways out of the role of the scapegoat, knowing full well that, in the end, you will have to discover, invent, and tailor your own way.

CHAPTER 2

The Story of the Scapegoat

Groups have long dealt with difference by blaming and exclusion. Examining the historical context of this can help illuminate how it works. Let's begin with a story that explains the origin of the name, *scapegoat*.

A group of bearded men in roughly woven robes gathers, chanting solemnly in the temple. The crowd parts as two male goats from the village herd are led, tethered and bleating, into the midst of the congregation. The rabbi intones a blessing as the first goat is brought before him. The rabbi reaches into a clay vessel and removes a marker. He reads the mark on the die and nods to his attendants. With a swift movement, he slices the goat's throat with his bronze knife while another priest catches the blood in an earthenware bowl. The singing continues as the rabbi walks into the inner temple, sprinkling the altar with the blood of the sacrifice.

Rejoining the congregation, the rabbi moves to the second goat and lays his hand upon its head. The goat's eyes widen in fear as the rabbi begins a slow and solemn recitation of all of the sins of the congregation. As he finishes recounting the ways that the group has failed their promises to a mighty and vengeful God, the goat bleats. A large man steps up and accepts the goat's tether from the rabbi. He leads the goat away from the chanting community of simple shepherds and farmers. Crossing the rocky ground, they travel farther from the encampment and deeper into the arid wilderness. At last the man unties the goat,

which bounds away into a bleak and uncertain future. The man shud-
ders with relief as he turns his back and heads home for the relative
safety of the oasis, each step putting distance between himself and the
"evil" and "polluting" contact with the goat.

The Old Testament describes a ritual of atonement for collective transgressions that involves two goats. Lots are cast. The goat that receives the "Lord's lot" (Lev. 16:8)[1] is slaughtered, and its blood is used to cleanse the "mercy seat" in the inner tabernacle. This goat pays for the sins of the community with its life. The goat that receives the other lot is the scapegoat. This "escaped" goat is spared from the knife. The Bible instructs, "And Aaron shall lay both his hands upon the head of the live goat, and confess over him all the iniquities of the children of Israel, and all their transgressions in all their sins, putting them upon the head of the goat, and shall send *him* away by the hand of a fit man into the wilderness" (Lev. 16:21).

The sins of the community are ritually dealt with in two ways. The first is by a blood offering that propitiates a vengeful God. The first goat's death allows the purification of the tabernacle for the appearance of the Living God, who will appear "in the cloud upon the mercy seat" (Lev. 16:2). Psychologically this is punishment and atonement without the redemption of continued consciousness—a kind of blind (unconscious) vengeance. Being dead, this goat can make no amends for its transgressions. Furthermore, its death is a nonspecific apology for sin. All that is required of it is its blood, and so amends cannot be directed toward particular, identified problem behaviors.

The fate of the scapegoat is different, and this difference has important symbolic significance. The *named* transgressions of the community are magically laid on its head, that is, guilt is *transferred* to the goat, and it is *banished* to the wilderness (a place where nothing human lives). So potent is this ritual decontamination that the "fit man" who leads the goat to the wilderness must carefully wash his clothes and bathe before he can reenter the camp. Even given the many admonitions in Leviticus about cleanliness and concern with ritual pollution, these passages stand out and represent the view (and wish) that a community's imperfections can be dealt with by transferring them to another and then excluding that member from the community.

Anthropologically there is ample evidence that the practice of scapegoating appears in cultures worldwide. Our word for medicine, pharmacy, comes from the Greek word *pharmakos,* which was the *person* who was ritually sacrificed to cleanse the community of sin and thus magically relieved the outbreak of pestilence in a city.[2] Ritual human sacrifice, particularly to appease angry gods, occurred throughout ancient Europe.[3] The rise of Christianity did not eliminate scapegoating in Europe, but only gave it a different look. The persecution of "witches," the Inquisition, and brutal sectarian violence were all undertaken in the name of the One True God against "sinful" others.

We need look only to the morning newspaper to realize that this process of naming, transferring, and banishing continues to this day. In the recent economic collapse in Korea, leaders of several failed corporations have accepted the blame for the country's woes, made public apologies, and accepted "banishment" to prison.[4] Although it may be true that their greed and mismanagement contributed to the financial crisis, it is noteworthy that their behavior is a culturally sanctioned phenomenon that seeks to localize the problems of a community, in this case of an entire economic system, as the failings of individuals.

Another topical example comes from the 1999 earthquakes in Turkey. The builders of many of the structures that collapsed with a subsequent tragic loss of life were vilified and punished. It is undeniable that many of them cut corners in construction materials and methods. It is also true that focusing exclusively on their greed and misbehavior allows the corruption of the local building inspectors, their governmental superiors, and even the bulk of the public who tolerated this system of bribery as a regular business practice, to go unmentioned. There is almost always some truth to the accusations against a scapegoat, but many other sins are laid against their name that rightly belong elsewhere. Punishing or excluding the scapegoat serves to relieve the system of the need to examine the structural problems of the system and of all concerned to explore their own participation in the problem. This ability of scapegoating to provide simple apparent "solutions" to complex problems is part of its power.[5]

What distinguishes scapegoats from other victims is their "specialness"—that is, that they are singled out to carry the blame for all. To be "chosen" can be very attractive, and this contributes to the difficulty that some scapegoats have in recognizing and reversing the practice. To be a "sacred victim" used to carry special rewards, such as food, sexual license, and prestige.[6] The one remaining social vestige of this is the sense of fulfilling an important group function. There are other, more psychological attractions that we will explore later, but one principle remains the same—the most powerful antidote to scapegoating and to being scapegoated is consciousness. That is, when we are aware of a pattern we can make choices. For instance, if we become conscious of how much the smell of fresh baked bread reminds us of pleasant childhood images of "home," we may be able to separate our emotional reaction and our rational assessment of a house that a realtor is showing us—especially when we know that realtors encourage such "homey" touches on open-house days.

Improving our information about a topic improves our ability to choose. Knowing that when pressure (whether it is plague in our village or the threat of merger in our company) increases in a system so does the likelihood of scapegoating gives us warning. This knowledge gives us a chance to avoid or interrupt the process of scapegoating.

In the next chapter, we look at the reasons that scapegoating is so powerful and so prevalent. But first consider how scapegoating can appear in our daily work life. We met Jack in the first chapter. Let's turn the clock back to understand how the process begins.

Jack was an intelligent and dedicated young professional who held himself and others to high standards of competence, effort, and personal integrity. He came to work in a new department and quickly established a reputation for hard work, attention to detail, and a quick wit. His supervisors gave him high marks on his job evaluations.

Over the course of the next few years, there were a number of changes in the company: upper management was reorganized twice, many new accounts were added, staff were expected to become "more productive," and rumors about a decline in the financial stability of the organization began to circulate around the water cooler.

Jack also heard rumors of a different sort: one of the managers was having an affair with one of the secretaries in the department; a colleague, Sally, had been reprimanded for taking home confidential business records; and another coworker, Bob, was leaving work early and falsifying his time card. One day Jack happened to encounter Bob as he was edging out the back door an hour before the close of business. Jack greeted him with raised eyebrows, and Bob hurried out, mumbling about needing to get to a doctor's appointment. Several days later Jack approached Bob and asked him if he was okay. Bob said he was fine. Jack told Bob he thought that he should know that there were some rumors circulating that Bob was not pulling his share of the load, and asked if Bob wanted any help. Bob said that he would handle it himself.

Management held a series of meetings to announce changes in the organization of the department and the work routine. They asked for

*employee feedback. Jack was outspoken about what he felt were ineffi-
ciencies and defects in the new plan. Despite having requested input,
the department head was obviously angry at having the plan openly
criticized. Jack politely asked if employee feedback was really welcome,
and the department head became angrier.*

*On his next job evaluation, Jack received low marks for "communi-
cation skills" and "team effectiveness." When Jack asked his immediate manager if this was retaliation for speaking against the department head's plan, he was told that it was more a reflection of his
"attitude." When Jack asked what would be evidence of improvement,
he was told that he was a "nitpicker" who took things "too seriously"
and was perceived as "judgmental" by other coworkers. When Jack
asked who held this view, he was told "many of the staff," but the manager refused to identify anyone. Jack indicated that this would make
it hard for him to know in what situations to change his behavior. Jack
also wondered how the same traits that had made him a valued
employee—diligence, attention to detail, and personal integrity—were
now seen as liabilities, but he kept his mouth shut and did not further
challenge his manager.*

*Over the next six months Jack experienced a marked change in his
work environment. Whenever he spoke in a staff meeting, the managers
would frown or sigh, and his coworkers would look away from him
nervously. He began to notice that although his coworkers still privately
sought his advice on projects, they were less likely to associate with him
when there were others around. In the lunchroom, fewer people would
sit down at the table where he was eating. When teams were being
formed for new projects that were in his area of special expertise, he was
not invited to participate.*

At this point, Jack was well on his way to becoming a departmental
scapegoat. We'll return to his story periodically, but let's first examine
the origins of organizational scapegoating.

CHAPTER 3

Groups, Troops, and Scapegoats

Why do otherwise decent people engage in scapegoating? The answer begins with the observation that human beings are social animals. Our evolutionary heritage includes many behaviors that help to establish us as members of a group. Whether our "troop" is a band of hunter-gatherers scouring the savanna for food or a platoon of soldiers on jungle patrol, powerful forces connect the group members and differentiate them from those who are nonmembers. Some of these forces are deliberate and conscious—like wearing a uniform—and some operate outside of our immediate awareness—like having shared the same "socialization" in basic training.

MEMBERS, NONMEMBERS, AND MOBS

Most creatures cluster in groups. Whether we think of an ant colony, a school of fish, a pack of dogs, or a nation state, we see that the odds of survival are greater when individuals are connected in a larger organization. Exclusion from the group is a powerfully stressful event for an individual, who will make vigorous and even frantic attempts to rejoin the group. Individuals who are unsuccessful in rejoining may exhibit disorganized and maladaptive behavior, and even appear to "give up" life-sustaining activities.[1]

This connection between group membership and survival accounts for some of the emotional power of scapegoating. To be ostracized—isolated from the group—greatly increases the individual's vulnerability (to predators, hunger, and illness), and so it is a powerfully fearful and aversive event. As people work and commute longer hours, their workplace assumes an even greater social significance. As they spend more time at work than with community or family, they become more dependent on work to meet their needs for group membership. This makes the impact of workplace scapegoating more powerful.

We have noticed that strong affiliation with a group outside the workplace—a community, church, social club, strong extended family, or even an athletic team provides some protection. If people have some other place where they feel they belong, they are better equipped to withstand workplace scapegoating. In chapter 8 we discuss the importance of forming "alliances" both inside and outside the workplace. But the general principle is to place your emotional "eggs" in several baskets, that is, to feel a member of several different groups, and not to identify completely with your career or workplace.

For many nonhuman species, birth is destiny—individuals are forever linked with the group into which they are born. Sometimes membership comes as a chemical "badge"—a scent that allows them to be recognized as a member. If they stray into another group's territory, it will also mark them as nonmembers and will precipitate attack and perhaps annihilation. Often though, the criteria of membership are more complex and consist of "performing" behaviors that signify they are part of the group. In primates, these behaviors can include rituals such as grooming or displays of dominance or submission. In human society, membership behavior is highly complex and can be as subtle as slight variations in linguistic pattern or accent.[2]

Human beings associate for many reasons, including kinship, proximity, and common interest. Social psychologists have long noted that group membership can be established through shared attributes (such as appearance), behaviors (including language), and values (shared beliefs or expectations). Paraphrasing the noted anthropologist-turned-psychologist Gregory Bateson, these are all "differences that make a difference."[3] They are distinctions that form a boundary between one group and another.

One of the ways in which we know who we are is to establish a boundary to know where we leave off and where the other begins. This may entail making clear statements of who we are *not*. Group rules or "norms" are often formed in opposition to the ideas that we have of others (e.g., "East Coasters are much more productive than those laid-back, latte-sipping West Coasters," or, conversely, "West Coasters do more creative work than those fast-talking, hostile East Coasters"). This process of "negative identity" formation can be readily seen in many adolescents who work hard to differentiate themselves from their parents by language, dress, and musical taste. This is a normal process, and dangerous only if one becomes frozen into asserting one's "differentness" solely by being "against" another. Assertions of "in-group" superiority ("We're the industry leaders, a lean and mean team") are also relatively harmless. Problems arise when group cohesion, or the appearance of group cohesion, is maintained primarily by opposition to or oppression of others.

The tendency for groups to define themselves in opposition to others is especially problematic when the "other" is seen as "less than," and hence not worthy of the same protections as group members. This is a common theme in wartime, when propaganda paints the enemy as less than human. Allied newspapers during World War I referred to Germans as "The Huns," and the reader can probably easily remember even more racist pejoratives from recent wars and conflicts. This is especially important given the power of social conformity—we tend to believe what everyone else believes.

There are numerous studies of the effect of social pressure on both perception and behavior. When confederates (secret associates of the experimenter who pretend to be fellow subjects in the experiment) all judge the shorter of several lines to be the longest, it is a very rare person who will persist with the perception that it is in fact the shortest.[4] However, having even one other person agree with your judgment makes it more likely that you will stick with it. Again this points to the importance of developing workplace allies who will help serve as a reality check on your perceptions.

Perhaps more troubling, though, have been studies that show that even ordinary people will behave badly toward others when instructed to do so by an authority figure.[5] People also quickly slide into hurtful behavior when they adopt roles that distinguish them from those whom they are hurting—roles that encourage an "us against them" mentality.[6]

In extreme form, we see the lack of individual responsibility in mob behavior. Note that adopting a role may or may not be a conscious choice. We may deliberately join a mob, glad for an excuse to cause mischief, or we may feel swept up in the emotions of the crowd, and only later reflect on what we have done. Crowd or mob behavior may be expressed in violence toward others, disorganized panic, or as apathetic "bystanding" to someone else's tragedy. All these are apparent in scapegoating: the readiness to gang up on the scapegoat, the fear of being contaminated by association with the scapegoat, and the reluctance to become involved in the scapegoat's suffering.

Social and political powers are often associated with group membership. This power represents a secondary, but important, motive for scapegoating. This power may come as economic gain, personal prestige, social privilege, or political office (which offers access to all of the aforementioned). Ambitious persons can capitalize on the human tendency to scapegoat in order to further these secondary goals. Consider how the case of Willie Horton (an African American felon who committed a brutal murder while on parole) was cynically used in campaign advertising to arouse fear (of African Americans) for political gain. Taken to an extreme by unscrupulous politicians, this leads to demagoguery and enormous human tragedy when different ethnic or religious groups are targeted as scapegoats. Recent examples include the Tutsis in Rwanda and the Albanians in Kosovo.

There are other reasons why scapegoating is such a pervasive phenomenon of group behavior. When the group is threatened, fear and anxiety can be reduced, and energy mobilized, by finding someone to blame. Sometimes this leads to useful change within an organization, but often the energy invested in blame causes more suffering than it relieves. Conditions that increase stress in a system (like overcrowding, the threat of layoffs, etc.) produce a fertile ground for blaming, and particularly for scapegoating—the naming, transferring, and exclusion of the blamed. There are many studies in nonhuman species that show that overcrowding and other environmental stressors increase aggression.[7] Social psychologists have demonstrated that human beings share the same propensity.[8]

A French philosopher, Renee Girard,[9] has suggested another theory to explain the prevalence of scapegoating in times of crisis. Briefly, he contends that in times of social unrest, the social hierarchy is disrupted, and particularly that *differences* (such as social class, position, or authority) between members of a society are obscured (as all members are subject to the cataclysm, whether it be a plague of unknown origin or a social revolution). Scapegoats restore a sense of difference, and hence of group membership.

We will have more to say later about the importance of "difference" and ways in which it can be dealt with in individuals and groups. But first, it is necessary to understand why scapegoating is so rooted in human social behavior.

BION'S THEORY OF GROUP DEVELOPMENT

During World War II, a young British Army psychiatrist, Wilfred Bion, headed a hospital unit for psychiatric casualties and was responsible for screening and selecting officers to lead various departments and missions. Trained in psychoanalysis, which was then the preeminent theory, he began to notice that knowledge of an individual's history and dynamics did not always predict his behavior in groups. In fact, groups seem to have almost a "mind" of their own. They seem to have rules and dynamics that powerfully influence the behavior of their individual members.

After the war, Bion went on to develop his ideas at the Tavistock Clinic in London, and evolved a theory of groups that is influential to this day.[10] Bion looked at groups both in terms of their rational, task-oriented behavior and their submerged "basic assumption" behavior. He theorized that all groups deal with issues that he labeled dependency, pairing, and fight-flight. The power of these "basic assumptions" comes not only from their universality, but also from the fact that in most cases, we are not aware of how they shape the behavior of the group.

Dependency assumptions relate to our tendency to look to a "leader" to solve our problems or to direct the group, much as children look to parents to care for them. Pairing is the unconscious promotion of alliances in the group to produce "couples" who will magically give birth to a solution to a group's problem. Fight-flight is the basic assumption that is most important for our discussion of scapegoating. The group actually forms around the themes of danger and opposition to a common enemy (who can be the group leader or a member who is seen as threatening group cohesion, problem solving, or who reminds the other group members of some unpleasant feeling).

Bion's work formed the basis for much of the modern work in group psychotherapy done in the United States, and the phenomenon of scapegoating in small therapeutic groups has been well documented.[11] A group can temporarily cope with anxiety by attacking one of its own members. The group becomes stronger and more cohesive through this attack, but ultimately it weakens itself because it obscures the real cause(s) of the anxiety. It is up to the group leader to help the group recognize this—and in the case of a therapeutic group, to prevent a scapegoated group member from being damaged emotionally.

One unnerving aspect of a "Tavistock group" experience is the initial silence of the group leader. This silence increases ambiguity and anxiety in the group, and begins to bring to the surface the "basic assumptions" that we described earlier, as various group members attempt to impose a structure on the group. When the themes of dependency, pairing, and fight-flight become visible in the group process, the members become aware of how previously submerged or hidden forces influence their behavior. They then are better able to make conscious choices about how they will act.

GUILT, SHAME, BLAME, AND SOCIAL COHESION

Human beings are fallible. We frequently fail to live according to the codes that we declare for ourselves. These include the laws of the larger society, the mores of our immediate social group, and the dictates of our religious or ethical system. Behavior that violates religious strictures is by definition sinful. Sin can be willful or accidental, but always represents an act (or a thought, which is also considered an act) that runs counter to the way that things *ought* to be, an affront to the *rightful* organization of the cosmos.

Some psychologists believe that the best way to understand social rules is to look at the ways in which families are organized. All families have rules. Some rules are explicitly stated—"Wash your hands before you eat." Some are not stated but are widely understood—"Dad doesn't have to wash his hands if he doesn't want to." Some are not stated and may not even be understood as rules—"If Dad doesn't wash his hands before Sunday dinner, the chances of Mom having a headache that evening increase dramatically." These unacknowledged rules are of particular interest because they often relate to emotionally important behavior. Playing by the rules, whether spoken or not, is one important way that we establish membership in a social group. Membership means being recognized by others as part of the group and of having the feeling of security that comes from belonging.

Many of the rules of the family have to do with the father. Whether this is rooted in our primate heritage (which values larger physical size and strength) or is an artifact of a patriarchal cultural history is open to question. For whatever reason, rules about the father have been the subject of many psychological writers. Freud interpreted much of the Old Testament as a disguised description of the murderous struggles between children (especially sons) and parents (especially the father).[12] Some analyses of the Book of Job[13] emphasize the themes of infanticide and (potential) parricide. Followers of the modern French psychologist Jacques Lacan suggest that everything we call the "law" is a symbolic manifestation of the Father.[14] In this view, transgression of the will of the father invokes the terror of castration or infanticide. While psychoanalytic theory emphasizes the importance of the fear of castration, the sad reality is that in human history, many more children have actually been killed than castrated.

Sociologists and anthropologists describe how social organizations develop a set of rules known as a "culture" which may be explicit (e.g., antisexual harassment policies, business dress codes, dress-down Fridays) or implicit (it's okay to flirt with the coworkers as long as you don't date them). Sometimes the rules also prohibit speech—for example, no personal phone calls from company phones or no proprietary information to be discussed outside of the company. Of special interest are the implicit rules that prohibit discussion—rules against talking about rules. Every family, workplace, or system has them. An example of this is Hans Christian Anderson's famous fable of the "Emperor's New Clothes"—only the poor peasant boy has the audacity to speak what everyone sees but dares not say, namely, that the emperor has been conned by some clever tailors and is proudly walking naked. The boy has named the unnamed, and in the story, fortunately for him, the crowd begins to agree.

It is important to know the rules of your workplace. This is called "surfacing the culture of the organization," and we explore this in detail in chapter 7. For now, think about what behaviors indicate "membership" in your company. Sometimes these emblems of membership are very concrete—like a security badge with your name, photo, and department, or a required uniform. Most times they are much more subtle and might include an unspoken dress code, knowledge of a special "language" (jargon, tech-speak, etc.), participation in rituals (an office football or lottery pool), and attention to an unspoken pecking order. Many of these rules are minor, and deviations are well tolerated though they may mark you as somehow "different" from the rest of the office.

In some companies, though, violation of the system's unspoken "rules," especially those rules about what may be said, when, and to whom, takes on the quality of sin—that is, transgression produces a powerful, negative emotional reaction in both self and others.

Central to the concept of sin is the notion of guilt—the offending party knows that s/he has "done wrong" and carries a dreadful feeling of alienation from the group—a sense of having "strayed from the path." For example, think about a time when you did something that violated your own sense of right and wrong—like not telling the truth to someone you love. You probably felt apprehensive at the thought of being discovered and found yourself replaying the event in your mind. You may have felt a bit awkward around the person to whom you lied and thought poorly of yourself. Guilt can be relieved by atonement, which is a combination of acknowledgment of error, punishment (penance), and a resolve to obey the rule in the future. Sometimes there is an explicit social ritual (like public confession) that restores membership "in good standing" to the community.

The idea of *individual* responsibility and guilt may actually be a relatively recent one in human history. Some psychologists claim that even the idea of the individual will is a fairly recent development, appearing sometime in the second millennium B.C.E.[15] The notion of collective guilt is much older.[16] Predating the Hebrews, the Babylonians describe rituals for atonement that resemble those described in the Bible in Leviticus.

It is likely that even older than the concept of guilt is the idea of shame. Shame is a social emotion that has to do with how we are perceived or *seen* by others in our social group. Shame is experienced when we are discovered by others to be violating some basic rule of the group. Imagine that you are at a fancy dinner party and give out a loud belch. Everyone stops his or her conversations and turns to look at you. Shame is characterized by a profound sense of embarrassment, blushing, and a desire to disappear or hide. Remember that in Genesis the first result of eating the forbidden fruit of the tree of knowledge is that Adam and Eve experience their nakedness and hurry to conceal it with fig leaf aprons (Gen. 3:7). In fact it is Adam's admission to God that he hid from God *because* he was naked that alerts God to Adam's disobedience. "And he said, Who told thee that thou *wast* naked? Hast thou eaten of the tree, whereof I commanded thee that thou shouldst not eat?" (Gen. 3:11). When we are deeply ashamed, we wish to hide our face from the view of others.

Shame always involves being seen by others as bad as having broken some important rule of society and as having been discovered or labeled unacceptable.[17] Scapegoating usually involves an attempt to shame the target publicly, as well as to induce a sense of guilt. Of the two, shame is primary, since it marks the scapegoat as different, or outside the bounds of the group. Scapegoating can be seen as a way of teaching the rules of the group, demonstrating the consequences of rule violation, and increasing group solidarity by banishing "otherness." It helps solidify a collective consciousness by locating what is undesirable in one place and excluding it from the group.

This phenomenon has been well studied by modern social psychology. Groups unite against a common enemy;[18] so one way to produce a cohesive group is to pit one group against another, or against an "other"—a scapegoat. The belief that the other poses some threat to the group increases the speed of group formation. The biblical scapegoat served to cope with the threat of group destruction by a mighty and highly vengeful God by separating the sin from the group of sinners. Not only does selecting a scapegoat increase the cohesion of the remaining members, it allows them to feel less afraid of the problematic attribute that is "isolated" in the targeted individual. They no longer have to consider that this attribute is part of their collective, or individual, mind. We explore this bit of psychological "magic" in the next chapter. Given these properties though, it is no wonder that scapegoating has such a pervasive and lasting appeal in human history. The tendency to scapegoat is always present. It is only by recognizing this that we can take steps to avoid being either victim or victimizer.

SUMMARY

People do things as members of a group that they might never consider doing as individuals. Social psychological experiments have shed light on group pressures for conformity, the effectiveness of threat in increasing social cohesion, and the transformational effects of being part of a "mob." These phenomena of group membership contribute to the creation of an "enemy" who is seen as different and "less than" the members of the group, making it socially acceptable to injure or exclude them.

Guilt, shame, and blame all play major roles in creating both social cohesion and scapegoating. Emotions have a social context and social rules governing expression. Understanding the "rules" is part of the basic human experience of developing in a family. Many of the rules of a family are unspoken, but are nevertheless powerful in shaping our behavior. Learning to look for the "rules" is crucial in understanding your workplace, and in avoiding scapegoating.

Social forces can be used to create a workplace atmosphere that actively promotes scapegoating. These forces are basic to social organization; thus, the tendency to scapegoat cannot be eliminated from human society—only the behavior can.

CHAPTER 4

Self, Psyche, and Scapegoats

Why do people become scapegoats? Why is it so difficult to recognize when it is happening? One very powerful way to understand how something works is to examine how it develops. So we will look at how people inadvertently slip into the role of the target, and along the way we will explore the individual origins of the human tendency to deal with unpleasantness by blaming and banishing others.

THE CONTRIBUTION OF DEVELOPMENTAL PSYCHOLOGY

Scapegoating involves projecting the unacknowledged or disowned aspects of the group onto the individual and then attacking him or her. In this way the unnamed can be named, blame "transferred," and the unacceptable attacked or banished.

Scapegoating also involves a kind of magical thinking that recurs in human history, which is recapitulated in the development of every human child. The elements of this "magic" have been the topics of academic developmental psychology for many years. How you come to know yourself as *self* (*identity*), how you cope with frightening information about yourself (*projection*), how you combine elements in perception and thought (*part-whole thinking*), and how you come to identify objects in your world (*naming or nominative functioning*) are all subtopics in the study of child development.

We will take a short tour through this world so that we can better understand why scapegoating is so prevalent and persistent in our lives.

The Formation of Identity

To understand this better, consider the world of the infant who is just beginning to differentiate *self* from *other*. The infant is simultaneously the *self* of the parents (quite literally formed from their genetic information, the tissues of their bodies, and the energy of their metabolism) and also the *other* (a dependent but also independent entity). Imagine that the parents, instead of cherishing and appreciating the "otherness" of their child, find this "otherness" extremely discomforting. In extreme cases they may even find it intolerable that the infant's will is not their own—for example, that the infant wants to relate when the parent wants to sleep or vice versa. Despite their best intentions, the parent may express disapproval or rejection. This communication may be subtle: a certain stiffness in the parental posture while holding the infant (described powerfully by the American psychiatrist H.S. Sullivan[1]); or it can take dramatic forms: an unwillingness to touch the child or even physical abuse of the child.[2]

How might the child react if this pattern were to be the most repeated experience of his or her social life? If, as Sullivan and others maintain, your sense of self is developed by generalizing the relational patterns that you experience, what are the patterns of relating to self available to this child? Building on the work of the early twentieth-century social theorist G.H. Mead, Sullivan stated: "Self is a reflected appraisal of others."[3] That is, you begin to know your "self" by adopting the behaviors (including the emotional responses) of significant social others toward your being. If your parents cannot tolerate your "otherness," it is unlikely that you will be able to either. Connection with parents is crucial to individual survival—and ultimately to the survival of our species. It is reasonable to believe that we will learn to do most anything to maintain this connection, even if it means adopting our parents' disapproval of our *self*. This becomes part of the "ground" of our being—an unquestioned attitude of belief in our own unworthiness. It creates a fertile field for identification with the role of the scapegoat.

If our "otherness" is not valued by our parents, and subsequently by ourselves, we are left with a lingering hunger to be "special" in some way. Sometimes we compensate by becoming so competent or so popular or so powerful that others must acknowledge us as uncommon and valuable.[4] Any of these paths leaves us vulnerable, since no amount of accomplishment is enough. As long as we seek validation externally, in the assessment of others, we fail to see that the answer lies in the acceptance of who we are. It is as if we were cooking our own meals according to another's appetite—sometimes we would get the food that we needed or desired, but at other times we would leave our own nutritional needs unmet. Until we recognize the reason for our "hunger" (and our ambition), setbacks or minor reversals of fortune are likely to be experienced as disasters, which throw us back to the infantile state of being "unlovable" and vulnerable to annihilation.

The child who has suffered this early socialization is likely to grow to an adult with an insatiable and cruel inner critic. This critic, who is an aspect of what psychologists call the superego, reviews shortcomings in excruciating detail, while glossing over real accomplishments. This stance exaggerates the "glass is half-empty" view of life: not only is the glass half-empty, but also it is that way because *you* were too dumb, too clumsy, or too slow to fill it, and, besides, *you* didn't deserve to have any in the first place. Perhaps worse still, this adult's accomplishments are not as satisfying as they could be. Since the acts were undertaken to please the parent, they represent the parent's desires (or what the child imagines the parent wanted) more than what the child wanted. The British psychoanalyst D. Winnicott calls this *the false self*. No wonder that the child/adult feels vaguely empty and dissatisfied. Many difficulties in living can attach to this structure, but the one we will focus on is the vulnerability to blame and its social manifestation, shame.

We have noticed that in the workplace, it is often the *overly* conscientious person who becomes the scapegoat. This makes sense both from the system's and the individual's perspective. Organizationally, the conscientious person may take a principled stand and speak the unspoken and unpopular. His or her words may be feared at the same time that they arouse envy, since what is overtly censured in organizations may be covertly valued.[5] Individually, the scapegoat may feel that *principle* (the "Law") requires him or her to speak regardless of personal cost, secretly enjoying the "specialness" of the dissenter's position. Some scapegoats may actually use their role to turn the rage that they usually reserve for their own scathing self-critiques outward, toward the organization. The negative reaction that they (quite predictably) experience not only provides the familiar experience of punishment, but also allows them the forbidden pleasure of righteously attacking someone besides themselves.

We believe that this scenario is especially true of a subtype of scapegoat that we call *The idealist*. However, there are many different paths to becoming a scapegoat. Some scapegoats are thrust into the role protesting loudly and clearly. Some wander into the role seemingly by accident. Each instance requires self-examination as part of the overall analysis. It is important to see that in some cases the scapegoat participates in her/his own persecution, for if the scapegoat recognizes this, he or she can choose to refuse the role.

If parents have trouble reconciling the complexity of their own emotional lives with the demands of society, they may cope with the forbidden feelings (often urges that are sexual, aggressive, or "against the law") by denying them, or by seeing them in others and attacking them. If they make their child the "vessel" for these warded-off feelings, the child carries the burden of being the unacceptable "other," and becomes primed for the role of the scapegoat, both within the family and, later, as an adult.[6]

Let's examine this powerful phenomenon, which is called projection, more closely.

Casting away Demons: The Power of Projection

There is another, more universal mechanism at work in scapegoating, and again developmental theory provides a useful perspective. This is the phenomenon of projection, that is, attributing a thought or act to another that rightly belongs to one's self. For example, a child of four or five years old may blame her doll for spilling the juice on the floor.[7] This is not done merely for social convenience—the child is absolutely convinced of the doll's guilt and *intention*. Thoughts as well as overt deeds are prone to this misattribution, particularly when the content of the thought is unacceptable to the thinker. Feeling furious with Daddy may be experienced as dangerous: *He's way bigger than me, what if he finds out that I'm mad at him?* And even against the internalized order of things: *Nice girls don't get mad, and I'm a nice girl.* Attributing one's unacceptable impulses to another temporarily solves both problems: *Daddy, watch out for monsters. They might eat you.* The tension created by thinking the "unthinkable" is reduced.

There are several problems with this solution. First, "unthinkable" thoughts may return, and again a suitable surrogate will have to be found and blamed. Second, it is not an accurate model of reality, so it can't serve as a model for effective action to address the causes of the unacceptable thoughts. That is, if the thought can't be owned, you can't say: *When you did X, I felt Y. I really wish you would do Z.*

Third, it creates a barrier to awareness of the origin of the thought, and so it isolates one part of the mind from the rest. Not only does this reduce the efficient functioning of the mind, but as we explore below, it also introduces errors of exaggeration and fluctuation, which are the products of this isolation.

Despite these shortcomings, projection is a mechanism of thought that remains throughout life, though thankfully supplanted in the course of normal development by other abilities that hold it in check. Still, when the adult mind is impaired—when we are very tired, intoxicated, ill, or stressed—projection is more likely to occur. A relatively innocuous example of projection occurs in daily life: Consider the traits that you find most annoying about your best friend. Is it possible that these are the traits that you most dislike in yourself, but that you don't wish to acknowledge?

Again it needs to be acknowledged that there is a grain of truth in most projections. That is, there often *is* something "wrong" in the other's behavior. The distortion is the *exaggeration* of the degree of culpability, and the silent and unnoticed way that undeserved "wrongs" are added to our assessment of the other. Most all of us have experienced what it is like to be the object of someone else's projections. It can be overwhelming to try to cope with the intensity of the disapproval directed our way. It can be puzzling to try to counter this disapproval, since the reaction is often disproportionate to our action. Sometimes projection leads to disaster.

> *George was a second-generation Arab American who moved his family into a new neighborhood. It was in a rough part of town, but it offered George a chance to own his own home. George was highly educated, spoke three languages, and had a graduate degree. He was used to getting a chilly reception from many of his countrymen, and knew that the Gulf War would probably make things worse—even though he was not of Iraqi heritage. He was not prepared for the hostility that he and his family received.*
>
> *His son was bullied in the nearby schoolyard. His car was vandalized in front of his house. He went to the school administrators to enlist their aid in setting up a meeting with the parents of the children who had bullied his son. The parents were unapologetic and suggested that he "go back where he came from." George pointed out politely that he came from Detroit. He visited his neighbors, taking them homemade jam from fruit he had grown in his backyard. He was active in organizing a block party to raise awareness about armed drug dealers operating on a nearby street*

corner. He was available when neighbors needed help starting a car or moving a refrigerator. Still many on his block muttered about the "A-rab" and claimed that he could not be trusted.

One evening as he sat eating dinner with his family, he heard a loud bang and then his dining room window exploded, showering him and his children with shards of glass. Thinking that someone was firing a gun at his house, he grabbed a pistol and ran outside. Seeing a young man drop to a crouch beside a parked car, George fired once, wounding the youth who, it turned out, was armed only with a slingshot. The youth recovered, but George was arrested and eventually was forced to move, selling his home at a substantial loss.

George was a victim of displaced anger and suspicion. His neighbors felt frightened and under siege from the local drug dealers. Beset by economic problems, many were barely hanging on to their own homes. George became a convenient target because he looked different from his neighbors, and because there was some implicit support from the larger society for directing anger at *Arabs*. His attempts to increase community togetherness—helping to organize the block-party, offering jam from his garden, and so on—were interpreted as further proof of his "different-ness." When he protested the mistreatment of his son, he was seen as a troublemaker. He was unable to break through the circle of projections that surrounded him, tightening around him and his family, and finally culminating in violence.

Mistaking a Tree for the Forest: Part-Whole Problems

One of the many contributions of Swiss psychologist Jean Piaget[8] is an increased understanding of how the concepts *part* and *whole* develop and operate in thought and in the perceptual field. Young children are more likely to focus on one aspect of a perceptual figure to the exclusion of other features. Piaget calls this process *over-centration*. This makes children especially vulnerable to some common optical illusions. Interestingly though, there are some optical illusions that are more likely to fool adults than children, and again this is because of over-centration. Adults look at some parts of the visual field (like the outline of an object) more than children do. If the illusion depends on this, the adult is more likely to be fooled. The invention of the eye-fixation camera, a device that allows researchers to plot exactly where a subject is looking as they examine a figure, has allowed empirical verification of Piaget's discovery that whatever aspect of a perceptual field is focused on, or *centered*, is likely to be overestimated.

Whenever we consider only one aspect of a situation, without placing it in the context of the rest of the perceptual field, we run the risk of overestimating its importance. When an employee voices a position that is disowned by the rest of the community, s/he risks being seen only for that position and not for the totality of her/his contributions. That is, there can be an overgeneralization of "badness" based on the intensity of the group's desire to disown the offending thought and an over-centration on the fact that the employee brought it up. The antidotes to this are first, to contextualize the dissent—that is, to place it within the larger perceptual field, say the overall goal of examining many possible courses of action—and, second, to bring attention to other "positive" contributions that the employee makes to the workplace.

Jane was a brilliant engineer with a somewhat direct and brusque personal style. She had alienated many of the other department heads by her frank, and sometimes scathing critiques of their proposals. When staff were asked their opinions about a new venture, she was openly scornful, pointed out a number of prospective pitfalls, and suggested an alternative plan. Her feedback was dismissed as yet another example of her "negativity" until one of her superiors approached the aggrieved department heads in private. He acknowledged that Jane's critique had been pretty harsh, but pointed out that she had been able to make accurate predictions in her home department, and that, after all, they had asked for "outside" assessments.

The plan was modified according to Jane's suggestion and was successfully implemented. While still somewhat unpopular, she gained the grudging respect of the department heads.

At the individual level, the employees being scapegoated may find it useful to notice their own tendency to "fragment," that is, to separate themselves into "good" and "bad" parts. Usually this results in the person focusing on the "bad" and hence overestimating it. Noticing that "parts" of oneself do not exist in real isolation can be helpful. That is, since at any moment we may show only a small fraction of our thoughts, actions, and feelings, we must be careful *ourselves* not to mistake the part for the whole.

Pete was feeling especially low about his work with a particular client, Mr. Wilson. No matter what he tried, the client found fault.

Pete's friend Mike listened to Pete complain about himself and his difficulties helping Mr. Wilson. He agreed that things did not seem to be going so well. He then asked how things had gone with the six other clients Pete had seen that day. Pete was taken aback, but complied. As he began to describe the other six, Pete saw that some were plodding along, and others were doing quite well. Pete began to feel better as he took a more differentiated view of his own work and of his effectiveness.

The Magic of Names

We are constantly constructing and revising our view or model of reality. Frequently we confuse this "map" with the actual "territory."[9] Ancient maritime maps used to carry elaborate drawings of sea monsters with the inscription *Sic hoc dragones* (Here be dragons) marking the uncharted waters. It is more reassuring to attribute a territory to monsters than to acknowledge our ignorance. When we don't know something well, we often invent a theory, and then behave as though the process of naming is the same as understanding.[10]

It is tempting to speculate on the origin of this phenomenon. We are all relatively powerless and vulnerable as children, yet language has the power to produce effects in others that extend our reach. This can happen quite literally when we learn, or invent, names for objects in our environment (like our bottle or our blanket), speak these names, and have others produce them for us. The "magic" of words is a deep-seated theme in myth and fairy tales. Remember that in the story of Rumplestiltskin, the evil dwarf is vanquished when the heroine is able to produce his name.

One of the great appeals of scapegoating is that it gives a *name* to our difficulty (as in *the Jewish problem*, *welfare queens*, or *problem employees*), as though this is a solution to economic or social problems. In the workplace, a host of ills, spoken or unspoken, can be added to the name of the "problem" employee, and the expectation is set up that if only something could be done about that individual, then things would return to normal, smooth functioning. This observation dovetails with the view of a modern theologian: *"Demonizing an enemy or oppressor gives courage to the vulnerable and a sense of power to the powerless* [our emphasis]."[11] This highlights another important function of scapegoating: the fact that taking some action, even if it turns out to be ineffective, or even magical, contributes to the experience of *mastery* and hence to the management of anxiety. We all do this when we are five years old, and we learn that words do have tremendous power to affect our surroundings and to manage the anxiety of being in the larger world. Why would otherwise reasonable people continue to indulge in this kind of magical thinking? The power that this magic retains into adulthood is due in part to its connection with processes that are out of immediate awareness.

The Tyranny of the Conscious Mind: What We Don't *Know* Can Hurt Us

Western psychology has always emphasized conscious, rational thought. In fact, it has become unfashionable and "unscientific" to maintain that important thoughts or feelings can occur out of awareness. Yet there are numerous everyday examples that we do just that. Consider the "tip of the tongue" phenomenon—trying to remember the name of the person in front of you whom you *know* you met at a party. You try to grasp it, but it eludes you, so you skillfully change the topic, and as you are earnestly discussing the new topic, the person's name springs to your lips. Clearly the "search" has continued out of your awareness and, in fact, was even impeded by your conscious attempts to remember it.

Freud's great contribution was his insistence that unconscious processes were influential and traceable in most behavior. Jung extended this view, elevating the unconscious mind to almost religious significance and warning that unconscious process could only be neglected at serious peril.[12]

One source of peril comes from the human tendency to simplify situations by equating new with known situations. That is, by carrying over or *transferring* patterns of feeling and relating what we have learned, usually in early childhood, into new situations where they may or may not be appropriate. For example, you may find yourself vying for the stern boss's approval with the same mixture of deference, fear, and resentment that you felt approaching your aloof father. Patterns that occur outside of conscious awareness are able to borrow the emotional power of earlier relations, and so take on an importance disproportionate to current realities.

Projection is a natural developmental tool for dealing with difficult interpersonal situations. It remains in your repertoire along with a number of other "magical" ways of thinking. If you believe that you have "outgrown" it, you are actually increasing the likelihood that it will be influential in directing your behavior. A thought out of awareness can become the "ground" of your experience—like the color of the wallpaper—subtly, or not so subtly, influencing your mood and limiting the range of possibilities that you consider. If the thought is not tied to emotional situations in which you have felt powerfully opposed or conflicted feelings, then usually it is enough to refocus and ask yourself, *Is there something here that I'm not seeing? Is there another way to look at this? Does this situation remind me of any that I've been in before?* Just voicing these questions is sometimes enough to open new ways of responding.

Sometimes, however, thoughts are more deeply submerged. If they are associated with painful feelings, thoughts are usually less accessible to consciousness. One theory holds that *isolation*—cutting off any aspect of the mind from the mutual regulating influence of the rest of the mind—is a sufficient explanation for the exaggeration and fluctuation that is often seen in maladaptive behavior.[13] If we cannot "own" a thought, idea, or behavior, then we cannot examine, evaluate, influence, or regulate it. This gives new meaning to the saying of the Roman playwright Terence: "Nothing human is foreign to me."[14] If we can consider the possibility that we, too, partake of what we dislike in others, then we are less likely to attack them as completely foreign and intolerably "other."

Often, though, we are not aware that we are the object of a projection. A particularly insidious version of this occurs when the projection touches our own self-accusation. It is in this instance that we are especially vulnerable to participate in the process of being scapegoated. Therapists have referred to this as the *scapegoat-identified* role. Adults who as children were regarded by their parents as intolerably "other" are prime candidates for a "career" as a scapegoat. Becoming dis-identified with the role requires becoming aware of situations where we "carry" (are the object of) projections. It also means becoming aware of the way that we contribute to the process, and this involves "taking back" or "owning" our own projections.

The identified scapegoat may be an unconscious partner in creating the drama of scapegoating. In some instances, the behavior of the scapegoat actually invites further scapegoating—it is as though both parties are locked in a spiral of conflict, and each attributes sole responsibility for the difficulty to the other. Please note that this discussion does not apply to situations where scapegoating is conscious and deliberate (some of the political and workplace examples that we have already mentioned). Deliberate scapegoating is a cynical power play and must be handled differently, as we describe later. To the extent that we are unaware of the "dance" that we do with our accuser, we are limited in our possible alternatives. We are "following the lead" of the accuser and actually helping to shape the form of the dance. When we become aware, we can try to change the dance, or leave the dance floor.

The forms of relating—the dances—are set fairly early in our social development. Usually they are variants of relationships we have had with socially important people (our "significant others") such as our parents, siblings, playmates, and teachers. Many of our favorite stories describe these relational templates. Cinderella and the Handsome Prince, Hansel and Gretel and the Evil Witch, and Beauty and the Beast are all common examples. The story of the heroine or hero overcoming great hardship to find happiness has tremendous emotional appeal. This appeal derives in part from connection to the dramatic roles that develop in our earliest social experiences.[15]

Let's return briefly to the story of Jack for illustration. But before we do, we want to caution against attempts to reduce or oversimplify scapegoating to the repetition or exercise of the scapegoat's early relational templates. Complex dynamics of an organization or *system* produce the actual phenomena that are scapegoating. The relational templates of the parties involved are only part of these dynamics.

Jack was the first child of lower-middle-class parents who worked hard to improve their social and economic condition. His mother worked as a teacher, but was studying to gain an advanced degree. Jack's dad was absorbed in trying to advance his career. Both parents were very busy and overburdened, and had little time to spend with him. Soon there were other children, and Jack, as the oldest, had to give up his "special-ness" as the only child, and was expected to take care of his younger siblings. He felt a "hunger" to be recognized, but many of his accomplishments seemed to be taken for granted by his parents. He was a sensitive observer, and quickly learned to recognize signs that he was pleasing others.

Both parents valued education, and Jack excelled at school. When he would bring home his report card, his parents would beam at the row of A's but would frown as they noticed a single B. "What happened here?" they would ask.

In elementary school Jack was bullied until he developed friendships with much bigger kids, using his quick wit to insinuate himself in their group. He became adept at deflecting verbal barbs with sarcastic humor. He relied on his powerful friends to protect him from physical attack. Jack became something of a crusader, arguing against the injustice of the schoolyard, trying to protect the smaller and weaker kids, and taking on "unjust" authority in the form of bullying peers and sometimes even bullying teachers. Occasionally he overextended his power. His friends would say, "His mouth wrote checks that his body couldn't cash." He suffered beatings and suspensions, but would continue to demand respect by his academic achievements and high test scores.

Jack did very well throughout his schooling, and entered the career world as a professional. After several successful jobs he joined the company where we first met him in chapter 1.

Because what we come to know as our *self* is formed in relation to important others, the form of these relations is so familiar and taken for granted that it is rarely questioned or examined. Since much of subsequent experience reinforces these relational patterns, they are remarkably persistent, even if they lead to difficulty—that is, even if the story has an unhappy ending. Jack began to prepare for a "career" as a scapegoat at an early age. He sought to please powerful and distant "others" by forcing them to acknowledge his competence, and by becoming conscientious and persistent, even if adherence to "principle" was costly. An important relational template was developed early: *he was the underdog struggling for recognition from and reformation of the top dog.* This template became activated at his work in a number of ways: first, when he saw evidence of "injustice" (Sally was reprimanded, but not the manager with whom she was having the affair; Bob was getting away with cheating on his timecard, etc.); and second, when he attempted to respond to the department head's invitation for constructive criticism. The department head did not recognize the value of Jack's contribution and behaved in a way that engaged Jack's need for acknowledgment and his dislike of hypocrisy. Jack responded by questioning the process, insisting on taking management's professed interest at face value instead of seeing it as a political strategy.

And so the cycle of escalating frustration was begun. Sociologists call this a *conflict spiral*, where the actions of one party trigger an escalated response from the other, and the other's response in turn triggers a more intense response from the first party, and so on. As we will see later, this pattern can be interrupted at several different points, and the cycle slowed or stopped. Again, for both individuals and organizations, the best remedy is awareness of the pattern and the conscious development of alternative stories (different relational possibilities).

If we remember that relational patterns always involve two or more characters, we can notice something very interesting—that both parties are necessary for the story to unfold as usual. Neither can play its part without the other. Because each role is a relational pattern, each contains the other. Implicit in each role is its counterpart. There can be no victim without a victimizer, no Hero without Villain. The scapegoat is a victim of accusation, but also an accuser of self and of others. And, to some extent, the accuser is also a victim and unaware of the attributes of which s/he accuses the other.

Making this process conscious reduces the likelihood of projection. In order to enact the drama, the usual story, individuals behave according to one side of the pattern and relinquish the other side of the pattern to the "other." If this "division of labor" did not occur, the story would be different. Many of the remedies that we will suggest in this book rely on recognizing when these patterns are happening and finding ways to "rewrite" the story.

Researchers have done some interesting work with bullies and victims of bullies in childhood.[16] They have found that most bullies were once victims of bullying, and that many victims also bully others. One way to cope with pain is to *pass it on*, that is to actively do to others what has been done to us. Jane Loevinger calls this process *reversal of voice*.[17] Bullies project their sense of humiliation and fear onto their victims, actively promote these feelings by behavior, and thus reassure themselves that they (the victims) are *not me*, that is, that they are not the crying child. This leads to some practical advice: *don't grovel in front of a bully, since it only accelerates the problem*. Similarly, the tendency of scapegoated employees to retreat, and to attempt to become "invisible," often adds to the perception that the criticism of them is deserved.[18]

There are a number of ways to cope with bullying. Most of us have had firsthand experience as kids at having been picked on and have probably used one or more of the following strategies: confrontation, alliance, or increasing the cost.

Confrontation means holding your ground in the face of attempts to bully you. Sometimes this involves fighting back. The key to this strategy is, win or lose, do not allow the bully to observe your pain, and, above all, do not beg or plead for mercy.

The second strategy is to make alliances with others, as there is power in numbers, or at least in a few large friends. In this scenario, the allies directly confront the bully. Since bullying almost always occurs with an audience, there is another, more indirect way that alliances can help. If enough bystanders are persuaded to protest the bullying, the bully is deprived of the attention and the increase in group status (even if it is achieved by inspiring fear) that reinforces such behavior. Many of the successful antibullying programs in schools make use of this strategy.[19]

The third approach is to increase the cost to the bully—make the difference between the satisfactions available from bullying and the expenses incurred from bullying smaller. This might mean fighting back directly or indirectly, not giving the bully the satisfaction of your tears or pleas, or in some other way letting the bully know that s/he needs to pick on a different target. This could include an appeal to "higher authorities" such as teachers or parents. In the workplace this might involve appealing to upper management, government regulatory agencies, or the legal system.

Another way of looking at the relation between bullies and victims is to focus on the way each is contained in the other.[20] The bully is also a crying child. This crying is intolerable, and so it is projected and attacked. It is more difficult to see that the crying victim of the bully includes the relational template of the bully. That is, the victim is capable of becoming a bully to others, and in some sense is already bullying him/herself by thinking badly of him/herself for not being physically able to overcome the external bully.

While it is natural to feel sad, fearful, and vulnerable when under attack, we are reminded of the words of a karate teacher we both knew, a short, mild-mannered gentleman who was a national collegiate champion in Japan. He said, "I can be beaten, but not defeated."[21] He meant, among other things, that he could lose a match, and even sustain a physical beating, but that his essential spirit remained untouched. It is possible to lose a battle and retain both your integrity and self-regard. A sense of humor helps achieve this, but also a recognition of your own participation in the process and your implicit power to affect feelings about yourself.

We explore this more in chapter 6, but first we'll look in more detail at how scapegoating happens in the workplace.

SUMMARY

The scapegoat takes on the aspects of a community that are disowned and even officially "unthinkable." The scapegoat is identified, blamed, and excluded from the community. The community—or workplace—temporarily gains cohesion and a sense of well-being. These gains are illusory, and the process of identifying a new scapegoat begins. This is a very old pattern, one that has been repeated many times in human history. It is maintained by powerful social and psychological factors, some of which gain their power by operating out of awareness,

Victims of scapegoating often inadvertently participate in this process. They may be repeating a familiar (and familial) role, they may feel important or useful, they may be validating a sense of unworthiness learned early on, they may experience the role as giving meaning and organization to their suffering, and they may be expressing forbidden emotions or knowledge.

Awareness of the process of scapegoating is the first step to developing the three effective strategies to counter it—confrontation, alliance, or increasing the cost to the bully.

CHAPTER 5

The Scapegoat in the Cubicle

Not all scapegoating is alike. There is some confusion and controversy among scholars about the scope of the phenomenon of scapegoating.[1] Some would limit the term to specific instances of religious ritual, whereas others consider that there are many different contexts in which it occurs, both consciously and unconsciously.

We think that it is most useful to define scapegoating in the workplace as one way in which *difference* is handled by individuals and organizations and that a typology of scapegoating can be developed based on the functions that it accomplishes and on the degree of awareness of the process. We will take a look at this process through the lenses of psychology, organizational systems theory, and theology. While some of the terms we use are borrowed from the original religious use of scapegoating, they are applicable to secular situations. We retain the terms because they convey the emotional power of this process.

THE ORGANIZATIONAL FUNCTIONS OF SCAPEGOATING

Every organization has to cope with *difference*. Differences might be as simple as those in appearance or as profound as deeply diverging business philosophies. When a company copes with difference by isolating, blaming, and excluding, the differences are by definition not integrated. Their value is lost to the organization, and a great deal of harm can be done to both the individual and the organization. We have identified four major motives for organizational scapegoating: cohesion, expiation, intimidation, and distraction.

Cohesion

As we saw in chapter 3, a group can accelerate its formation by defining itself in opposition to others. Finding or creating a "common enemy" is a rapid way to produce in-group cohesion. All else being equal, we might expect to find this kind of intolerance of difference in a workplace that is newly organized.[2] Existing organizations can also be gripped by this "fight-flight" dynamic at times of organizational stress or change.

> *Shirley started as a long-distance operator at the phone company twenty years ago and had worked her way up to a middle management position. The phone company went through several reorganizations, some forced by governmental regulation, some by attempts to become more profitable. Now another reorganization loomed, and Shirley was told that her department was being "consolidated" and that she could relocate to a distant community or she could accept a lesser position in another department. Because she felt strong ties to her community, she chose the lesser position.*
>
> *But as soon as she started, she began to feel trouble brewing. Her new supervisor found fault with everything she did. Shirley felt that he watched her every move, and that he never missed an opportunity to criticize her in front of other workers. She felt humiliated and that she was being used by her supervisor to "make points" with upper management. She made some discrete inquiries and found out that her supervisor's previous department had also been "reorganized" and that he and about half of his old department had been transferred to the current work group. He had been faced with the challenge of blending other transferred employees with his own into a "new team."*
>
> *She could appreciate the difficulty of this, and she also suspected that he saw her experience and competence as a challenge to his authority as the head of this new work group. She approached him privately and sympathized with the problems of integrating displaced workers into a new group. She made it clear that she had a stake also in making sure that this transition went smoothly and offered her assistance. She raised the idea of "team building" activities, being careful to do so in a way that let the new manager take credit for the ideas. Over the course of the next few weeks, the harassment ceased.*

Shirley had exceptional social skills. We discuss some of these later in chapter 9. But none of her skills would have helped had she not "diagnosed" the problem correctly, namely, that her manager was anxious to develop group cohesion (as well as to assert his authority) and that his way of doing this was to set up a disapproved "other" (Shirley).

This method of creating group cohesion "works"—it does increase cohesion—but it does so at great cost. The cost is measurable in human suffering, and also in the loss of diversity to the organization. If membership in the "in-group" requires narrow conformity, the organization has fewer ideas, skills, and resources to cope with a rapidly changing environment. Just as planting all your fields with one variety of corn leaves you vulnerable to pests that are specific to that crop, or vagaries in the weather, having organizational "sameness" makes it more difficult both to compete in a world that is diverse and to adapt to change.

Expiation

Expiation is the process of making amends for guilt. Guilt for error is admitted or assigned, and some penance is undertaken to expiate or "pay for" the error. It is a way of assigning responsibility for a problem to an individual or group, and in that way *absolving* all those who are not that individual or group from responsibility for the problem. No one likes to feel that s/he has made an error. Blaming allows a sense of distance from this feeling, and by locating the blame in the "other," a sometimes-magical sense of control is gained. That is, if we know that it is someone else's fault, we feel that we "know" more about the problem and that we are somehow closer to the solution. We can present ourselves to others, including our managers, as having "done something." Sometimes this is accurate. Most often it interrupts the search for a real solution.

If the problem can be located in individuals, it may seem logical simply to replace these individuals. This may produce some short-run relief, but it also may obscure systemic problems. The need for expiation is particularly strong in workplaces that have established a culture of "blame" or that deal with powerfully emotional issues such as life and death. The health care industry is a prime example. People's lives are quite literally at stake, and errors are expensive in both human suffering and monetary terms. A hospital's "morbidity and mortality" conference is an attempt to *separate* understanding and blaming—in the conference, all aspects of a case are examined with a goal of improving practice rather than punishing mistakes. A similar approach has been advocated in the airline industry for understanding crashes and near misses.[3]

If we decide that understanding is more important than blaming, it may be easier for people to come forward with the information that will enable us to devise solutions for problems. When our emotional investment in blaming is high, the need for expiation is great, and the pseudosolution of scapegoating may replace the more difficult search for real solutions. The higher our level of anxiety about being blamed, the more likely we are to attempt to fix blame on others.

A nonprofit alternative educational institution suffered chronic cash-flow problems and was undecided about the advisability of trying to expand in order to take advantage of economies of scale or to remain in a "niche" market. The school went through a series of presidents, each one leaving under a cloud of financial crisis. The board made decisions with little involvement from the faculty or students, each time convinced that their new choice of chief executive would resolve the problem. Executives were demonized and discarded in favor of new and more powerful executives. Ultimately the character of the original institution was transformed into something unrecognizable, while the structural problems—including the relation of the board to the actual purpose and daily functioning of the institution—were never addressed.

It is important to note that we are not arguing against individual accountability. We are all responsible for our actions and for fulfilling or renegotiating our commitments. Employees must have the power as well as the responsibility to complete a task. Scapegoating often occurs in situations where there is an illusion of power. That is, in a situation that is impossible for the scapegoated individual to solve.

Physician A worked successfully in a group practice for a number of years. As the nature of health care reimbursement changed, the group experienced great pressure to work "faster" in order to improve access without increasing staff. Physician A continued to try to spend time with his patients and was ostracized by his colleagues, who began to subtly impugn his competence, integrity, and work ethic. This allowed them to continue to pretend that they were providing the same quality care to their patients and to avoid discussion of the impact on their own practices of the economic changes. It also made it difficult for them to explore creative solutions or to cope with the sense of loss that most of them experienced. Disability premiums for the physicians in this practice went up 300 percent in one year.

Organizational specialists have coined the term "surplus powerlessness" to describe work situations in which staff feel helpless to alter the course of their work lives.[4] When the sense of being powerless increases, people can cope in a number of ways, including increasing their problem-solving attempts, retreating and isolating, or becoming demoralized, protesting, and blaming. When blaming increases, so does the likelihood of scapegoating. The ills of the organization can be transferred to an identified "problem employee" and banished, thus "expiating the sin" of the group. Because the scapegoat's total responsibility for the problem was illusory, so is the solution.

Intimidation

A third function of scapegoating is to silence the protest that can accompany organizational unrest, especially in situations of "surplus powerlessness." If it is clear that dissent leads to blaming, isolation, and banishment, people are less likely to express differences openly. There is an old Japanese saying that "The nail that stands up is the one that gets hammered down." If employees see a coworker "hammered down," they may respond in a number of ways: they may be openly supportive, they may be publicly silent but privately supportive, they may retreat in fear, or they may actively cooperate with the stigmatization of the identified target.

It is this last response that is most relevant to our discussion. Colleagues may convince themselves of the correctness of the criticism of a fellow worker in order to preserve their sense that the workplace is "fair." Social psychologists call this phenomenon "cognitive dissonance."[5] The more invested employees are in believing that their workplace is "fair" (and the more frightened they are to acknowledge that it isn't), the greater their need to believe that the criticism of the targeted employee is accurate, and the more likely they are to notice other flaws in the target's performance.[6]

Outright fear of contagion may also cause colleagues to avoid the target. That is, if they are seen to associate with the target, then they may also become targets. This contributes further to the employee's isolation. The isolation may be seen as "proof" of the fairness of the criticism—that the target is in some way intolerably different and deserving of isolation. Again the process is identification, transference of blame, and banishment—the now familiar career of the scapegoat.

Organizationally, intimidation can be used consciously or unconsciously to limit dissent, to induce conformity, and to keep employees fearful and obedient. It can be very effective for these purposes. It is also extremely corrosive of morale and discourages creativity and flexibility at a time in the history of work when these may be the most valuable assets an organization can have. Managers who care about these assets need to take particular notice of how scapegoating happens. Employees need to protect themselves, each other, and even their managers from the negative impacts of scapegoating. In order to do this, employees may need to learn to "manage" their managers. A large part of this reverse managing depends on an accurate analysis of the situation and the motives.

If scapegoating is being done as a deliberate intimidation tactic, it usually means that it has strong institutional or cultural support. If this is so, the *only* solution is collective action. There is no effective way that a targeted individual can cope on his or her own except to find employment elsewhere. We discuss this further in chapter 7. If, however, the intimidation is unconscious, or even accidental, making the pattern conscious *may* be sufficient to alter it. Differences can be recontextualized as "thinking outside the box," or "diversity of opinion and skills," and so on. Appeals can be made to common purposes (creative solutions, loyal opposition, the devil's advocate, etc.). The negative consequences of stifling dissent or punishing nonconformity can be raised skillfully.

In a closed meeting, management asked for line staff input on a prospective hire. Mary raised concerns about how the prospective employee's stated interests appeared to be a mismatch with the department's needs. The chief manager dismissed her concerns brusquely, saying, "Well, of course, I knew you would say that, but I wanted to hear what others have to say." The rest of the staff quickly raised even more serious objections to the prospective hire, and did so with some humor. Had they also added, "When you ask for input and dismiss it, it's hardly an encouragement for people to help," they could have expressed their opinion not only on the immediate issue, but also on the way in which dissent had been marginalized by being located in a single "malcontent" employee.

The most insidious intimidation is one that connects with the target's own unconscious fears or issues. That is, when a manager senses employees' relational templates and attempts to use them to control or scapegoat. The manager may not be fully aware that s/he is doing this, but the manipulative potential is high and the effect highly intimidating. Let's return to Jack.

Jack had been openly critical of changes in office policy and had presented both a rational critique of the policies and some constructive alternatives. His department head, Frank, told him that he wanted to speak with him, but was then unavailable for a meeting for a week. Jack's anxiety began to rise. He sought out a trusted colleague, Mike, who told Jack that it was dangerous to approach this meeting with the manager with the attitude that he (Jack) needed to placate Frank. Specifically Mike had noticed that Jack had previously sought approval from Frank almost as though the manager (an older male) was his father. Mike reminded Jack that he was unlikely to get "the blessing of the father" from Frank, and that in fact, Jack had only spoken things that many others in the office had felt as well.

On the day of the meeting, Frank began in a solicitous voice to say how concerned he was that Jack seemed "so unhappy" in the office, and wondered if he would be happier working someplace else. Because Jack had become aware of his own pattern, he was able to silently decline this ploy (of false sympathy) to induce him to resign, and to calmly restate his concerns about the policy changes. He did not participate in a redefinition of the issue as being his personal problem. He acknowledged that he was not happy about the changes, but he aligned himself with the manager, stressing their shared desire that the department operate well and offering suggestions as to how this might be accomplished, while acknowledging that the manager was responsible for making the final decisions. Frank continued to be wary of Jack, but soon picked other staff on whom he focused his displeasure.

It is up to the target to become aware when this situation is occurring. Some of the warning signs of this kind of intimidation are changes in feeling. While it is natural to be anxious if the boss is displeased with you, a high degree of distress may indicate that an old, archaic relational pattern is at work. If you are feeling vague, ill-defined, but intense feelings that *something is not right*, you are probably correct. Consulting with friends or professionals can help you get a "reality check." If you can locate your own contribution to the situation, you can better understand if you are being intimidated by your boss, by your own history, or by both.

There is a subtype of intimidation that is noteworthy, namely, using a scapegoat as an "example" to others. In this variant, the scapegoat is not banished entirely, rather s/he remains with the organization, but usually in some diminished or debased capacity, as a kind of cautionary tale for what can happen. Scapegoats may be perennially passed over for promotions, raises, or bonuses. They may be moved to smaller offices or less desirable cubicles. They may have most of their job responsibilities given to others, and be given only trivial or especially boring tasks. Yet they serve an important organizational function. They are a warning to other employees about what *can* happen if you *stray from the path* of conformity to the expressed and implied rules of the organization.

Distraction

When energy is focused on the real or supposed ills of a targeted employee or scapegoat, several things occur. As has been mentioned, identifying a scapegoat causes the members of the community to believe that they have located the source of the problem, and so the search for solutions can stop. Also, a manager who feels vulnerable may look to shift attention to a "problem" employee in order to distract from his or her own weaknesses.

> *Allen was a middle manager who busied himself with numerous "special projects" while often letting his more mundane (but essential) tasks slide. He began to accuse his employee, Bob, of not keeping up with the routine and required documentation of work performed. In fact, Bob did a lot of work, though he was slow to document it. Allen counseled Bob about the necessity of documentation, and Bob agreed that he would improve his performance. Allen continued to monitor Bob's documentation closely, and to complain to others in the office about the lack of it. Allen spent a lot of time and effort documenting Bob's lack of documentation, and finally "wrote him up" (disciplined him). Allen's own routine work continued to be neglected, but the attention of the office was on Bob.*

The process of scapegoating consumes time, energy, and emotional resources, so the actual capacity of the system to consider alternatives decreases. When we look in the wrong place, it is no wonder that it is difficult to come up with creative solutions. For all these reasons, scapegoating is an inefficient problem-solving method. But its power to redirect attention makes it a powerful tool for managing organizational dynamics. If there are factions within management that want to remain free from scrutiny, they may use scapegoating, of individuals or even of other departments, to exhaust the organization's ability to self-observe and problem solve in a full and conscious fashion.

> *Marketing had overpromoted a high-tech product and knew that it would not be able to deliver to specifications by the promised release date. And so marketing began a campaign of blame against one specific work group in the research and development (R&D) department. The head of this department was slow in investigating the concern and in defending the work group. Ultimately there was such pressure from upper management—who had been hearing primarily from the marketing department—that the head of R&D disbanded and dispersed the work group rather than face the ire of upper management. Marketing's role in creating the problem was never examined.*

While this seems an extremely crude strategy it is often effective. Think of how a stage magician uses distraction, redirection of attention, and the power of expectation (we often see what we expect to see and look where we are told to look) to create vivid illusions. This can happen in subtle ways as well. We are used to the idea of individual responsibility, but sometimes it, too, is an illusion. Sometimes we as individuals do not have the power to effect change. This can be a very frightening realization, and one that many of us would rather not make. Instead, it is easier to blame ourselves or someone else for an error. When we do this, we distract ourselves from the real problem, which is our powerlessness.

During the Middle Ages in France, the Jews were blamed for outbreaks of the plague.[7] Although this rightly seems barbaric if not insane to modern readers, even relatively well-educated people believed this at the time. Powerless through ignorance of the real causes of this illness, they dealt with the terror of sudden and horrible death by blaming, dehumanizing, and murdering others.

When Rwandan Hutus blamed Tutsis for the economic stagnation of their nation, they ignored both the governmental corruption and global financial policies that are very difficult, if not impossible, for an individual to effect. But since Tutsi individuals were visible and available targets, within easy reach of machetes, demagogues could divert attention from their own participation in the economic corruption, and tragedy ensued.

Much less dramatic examples exist in the office or factory. When economic forces induce companies to lay off workers, managers, or personnel, department staff may be demonized. It is much easier to be angry at an individual than at a system that behaves as though workers were interchangeable and disposable. It is also much harder to imagine how to begin to change such a system.

Still, if attention is diverted away from the system and onto a few individuals, it may be impossible. The French poet Baudelaire once said, "The Devil's cleverest trick is to persuade you that he doesn't exist." We believe that the devil's cleverest trick is to persuade us that he exists as a discrete *individual*, and not as a part of every person and system.

CONSCIOUS AND UNCONSCIOUS SCAPEGOATING

Just as individuals may or may not be aware that they are projecting a disowned thought or feeling onto another person, organizations may or may not be aware that they are locating blame on an individual that rightly belongs to the group. When workplace scapegoating occurs consciously, it is a deliberate ploy or strategy to gain power, deflect blame, or avoid scrutiny, as in the cases of Allen and Bob and the marketing versus the R&D work group. Although conscious scapegoating may seem like another tool of the powerful, often it is a sign of their weakness. It certainly should alert us to investigate what is being avoided, that is, to look for what issues the scapegoaters are trying to hide or confuse. Whenever a manager (or a politician for that matter) is trying to convince us that *all* of the group's problems are due to one or two "problem" individuals or classes, look again. The problem may lie in the way that work is structured, in the communication channels between levels of management, or in the career agenda of the person who is trying to use scapegoating to inflate his/her perceived value to the company.

Individual managers or coworkers may deliberately set up others to fail in order to disprove a theory or to make a point. If they consistently single out one individual, citing this person's "history of failure" (which they helped create), then they are scapegoating. We know this pattern by its common name, "The Fall Guy"—when criticism looms, make sure that it falls on someone besides yourself. Making someone else look bad so that you look good by comparison is a common strategy for advancement in an organization. Sensible organizations look to the overall functioning of the company and thus avoid this trap. Unfortunately not all organizations are so sensible.

Sally was a secretary at a large public university. She took a job in a new department as an administrative assistant. She was so excited about the increase in pay and responsibility that she failed to follow her usual procedure of exploring why the previous person who had held the position had left. In fact, none of the last three people who had held the job had stayed more than six months, the university's "probation period." Her immediate supervisor, Jane, greeted her warmly, and told her that part of job duties would be to "be her best friend." Sally thought that she was joking. It soon became clear to Sally that although Jane was an intelligent and capable woman, she expected Sally to carry the bulk of the work of the office and to listen to her complaints about the faculty, the other staff, and her own husband. Sally tried to accommodate Jane's every request but became increasingly resentful. She tried to extricate herself from some of the personal conversations Jane initiated, citing the mounting pressure of undone office work. Jane became increasingly critical of Sally's "inefficiency." Sally became flustered and began making mistakes. The efficiency of the office declined, and some faculty complained. Jane, responding to criticisms of the office, went to the departmental supervisor with complaints about Sally. Since Jane was a veteran, and Sally a timid newcomer, it was easy for the departmental supervisor to agree with Jane and to blame Sally. Sally eventually left for another job but not until after a great deal of threats, unpleasantness, and loss of self-esteem.

When scapegoating is conscious, it has the quality of bullying. As you remember from our discussion of bullying in chapter 4, there are several ways to counter bullying: confrontation, alliance, and increasing the cost to the bully. All these can be combined to convince the bully that his/her purposes will not be well served by continued efforts to scapegoat. The bully can then make a conscious and "rational" calculation (rational in the sense that economists use this term) that scapegoating is not going to work, and other means to a desired end need to be explored or developed. When the process of scapegoating is unconscious, or not part of a thought process, this calculation can't be made, and different means are necessary to interrupt the cycle.

When both parties to the process (the blamer and the blamed) are unaware, the conflict between them has a quality of inevitability, escalation, and familiarity. They are locked in a relational pattern that has roots in their own individual psychologies and in the society at large (the collective consciousness). The story of Jack that we have been following is an example of a situation where both sides to the conflict were initially unaware of the pattern. Jack is a type of scapegoat that we call "The idealist," and the organization of his workplace supports scapegoating for intimidation, distraction, and, to a lesser extent, expiation.

Since the workplace is organized for a specific purpose (the production of "work"), it may actually respond better than individuals to efforts to make it aware of its own organization. There is a vested interest in the efficiency of the system (which translates directly as profit), and if it can be demonstrated that scapegoating is an inefficient way to cope with difference, there are powerful natural allies for change.

Making the unconscious pattern conscious also gives the individual some warning about the progression of the situation at work, and allows room to consider other options. If we are headed down a familiar highway, we may not "wake up" until we have already passed our exit. Becoming and remaining aware of relational patterns is a lot of work, but can save a lot of backtracking and frustration.

THE CAREER TRAJECTORY OF THE SCAPEGOAT

Just as scapegoating can serve different organizational functions, there are different paths for individuals to arrive at the role of the scapegoat. Some of these paths are related to larger societal processes (like the devaluing of the feminine), some to issues of individual psychology (like the idealistic "whistle-blower"), and most to some combination of these (see the "underdog/top dog" relational pattern). Scapegoats, like any other employee, have a progression to their "career." All the different types of scapegoats share the same basic three-stage process: *identification* (being singled out), *transference of blame* (projection), and *banishment* (isolation and attack). Understanding this progression is important, because it has implications for how the cycle can be interrupted.

Identification

The first step in the process is identification of a target for scape-goating. This may involve an active search by the community for a scapegoat or by a target "volunteering" for the role. Active searches need not be conscious. An organization or community may not ac-knowledge that it is looking for someone to blame, but may none-theless begins to notice who in the group is "different." Differences may be readily apparent (gender, skin color, manner of speech or dress, etc.) or more subtle (religion, politics, personal style, sense of humor, social skills, etc.). In times of organizational stress, the attribution of difference may become an opportunity for blame.

Systems will sometimes probe for difference. That is, group lead-ers may present members with various "tests" of performance, style, or loyalty to begin to separate and divide the group.[8] More subtle versions of this include giving favorable treatment to one or more employees and observing the reactions of the others, or, conversely, increasing the workload on a single employee to see how both that employee and others around him/her will react.

When differences are more difficult to identify, they may be manu-factured. For example, an organization may begin to keep statistics on employee "productivity," which may or may not reflect the actual amount or value of work accomplished. These statistics are intended as markers of difference between employees and already carry implicit value statements (i.e., more is better). These markers can easily be-come the basis for blame and scapegoating.

Sometimes an employee will inadvertently begin the process of scapegoating by openly challenging management or coworkers (sug-gesting that s/he is willing to "stand out"), or by repeatedly seeking reassurance that s/he is doing a good job (implying a lack of confi-dence about his/her own performance). While coming from differ-ent motives and psychologies, each of these behaviors marks the individuals as *different*, and difference can then become a target.

There are various ways of "volunteering" for the role of scapegoat. Employees can simply "nominate" themselves by being perceived as different, or they can actively participate in the process of escalating the conflict. When old relational patterns are set in motion, this esca-lation can happen quickly and be difficult to reverse. This is why it is important to understand your own participation in the process.

Transference and Escalation of Blaming

It is rare that workplace scapegoating begins at high intensity. Usually it starts with criticism of performance or "attitude." If this criticism is given directly, the target can evaluate its accuracy, accept it constructively if it is deserved, or politely contest it if it isn't. Contesting inaccurate criticism may reduce targeting and future blame. But it may also serve to further differentiate the employee, especially if the manager is not used to anyone expressing a differing opinion. "Managing" your manager becomes important here. It may be most effective to leave him or her a face-saving way out. We say more about how to do this in chapter 8.

If the criticism is indirect—such as a manager complaining about one employee to another employee or coworkers gossiping about a peer—there is much more room to escalate the blame by "adding on" other supposed transgressions. This escalation is more difficult to counter as it often has developed momentum before the target ever becomes aware of it. The best defense here is advance preparation. If you have already made "alliances" in your workplace, it will be much harder to isolate you. Again we explore particular ways to do this in chapter 8.

Retaliation and Self-Fulfilling Prophecies

There are several ways in which the process of isolation and blame become recursive, that is, how each reinforces the other, escalating the conflict.[9] In one, the target, sensing that something is amiss, may begin to protest. This protest may be seen as "proof" of guilt. If the protest is delivered in a hostile or angry fashion, outside observers may focus on the form rather than the content of the communication and agree that the blame is deserved.

> *Sarah was a medical technician who began work in a new clinic. She came into a department that had a closely knit group of technicians. This closeness was accentuated by their shared ethnicity and language. Sarah was the only "outsider." She felt uncomfortable when the other staff would look at her and speak to each other in a language that she did not understand. But she tried to fit in, often assisting her coworkers in taking care of their patients.*
>
> *The clinic set time limits on care. Each technician was supposed to process a new patient every fifteen minutes. Sarah was conscientious and often took the full fifteen minutes with a patient, making sure that all*

procedures for care had been followed. As a consequence management saw her as being "slow." Even though she had frequently helped the other techs with their patients, when one of the techs tried to help Sarah out because she was running behind schedule, the other techs told her not to help. Sarah felt excluded. She went to her supervisor, who advised her to "just ignore" the slights from her coworkers, telling Sarah that these were just "cultural" differences. The supervisor, thinking to make Sarah's work easier, or perhaps wanting to avoid a potentially unpleasant confrontation, put Sarah to work alone in a different part of the shared work area. This made Sarah feel worse, as her coworkers began to spread rumors about Sarah's ability to do her work, and would stop speaking to each other in English as soon as Sarah came near. Sarah again went to her supervisor, who then expressed exasperation at Sarah's "sensitivity."

Sarah's story illustrates a variant on the basic pattern: the blamers set increasingly high standards of performance, while withholding the resources needed to meet the goals. This results in a higher likelihood of failure, which becomes further "evidence" of the target's blame-worthiness.

Banishment

Banishment of targeted individuals may be literal. They may have their employment terminated directly and be given an hour to collect their personal possessions while a security guard watches and then escorts them off the premises. Or banishment can take symbolic forms as the scapegoat is allowed to continue employment but is isolated, moved to a different location, stripped of signs of prestige, given less meaningful work, passed over for bonuses, and so on. Once scapegoating has reached this level, reentry as a regular member of this workplace community is almost impossible.

SUMMARY

Scapegoating serves at least four major functions in organizations: cohesion, expiation, intimidation, and distraction. Cohesion can be increased (temporarily) by creating an "in-group" (the "good employees") and an "out-group" (the scapegoated employee[s]). Expiation provides some relief of the shame and guilt that accompanies error. Intimidation provides control through fear. Distraction provides control through the redirection of attention. These functions can be satisfied consciously or unconsciously. That is, they can be deliberately undertaken, or they can occur out of awareness. Different strategies for countering scapegoating are needed, depending on the functions that scapegoating serves in the system.

In the workplace, scapegoating involves identifying, blaming, and excluding. In order to plan effective countermeasures, it is necessary to understand the factors operating in a particular instance. This requires understanding how individuals interface with organizational functions to produce scapegoating, and we look at this phenomenon next.

CHAPTER 6

Idealists, Realists, and Scapegoats

A TYPOLOGY OF SCAPEGOATS

In most situations scapegoating is the result of complex factors in both the organization and the targeted individual. In general, we think it is preferable to focus on the principles (such as projection, distraction, intimidation, etc.) inherent in the way organizations cope with difference rather than identifying types of scapegoats. Still, typologies are often useful in helping us to locate and identify factors that give each instance of scapegoating its particular shape. So we examine some of the different subtypes of targeted scapegoats to explore their individual contributions to the problem. Again, it is important to keep in mind the relative power of the participants so as to avoid the temptation to blame the victim of scapegoating.[1]

The Idealist

The idealistic scapegoat is willing to pursue a principle, like fairness, even if it results in conflict with workplace authorities. Idealists will sacrifice their own immediate interests in order to maintain their integrity, their view of who they are. These are the "whistle-blowers" in an organization. Jack is an example. His strength is his willingness to state the implicitly forbidden. Idealists can restore balance to a system by articulating perspectives that may be being ignored. In politics they are "the loyal opposition," and serve as a check on over-enthusiastic or shortsighted policies. The Quakers in eighteenth-century England embodied this role of "speaking truth to power." Enlightened workplaces value the input of this type of difference.

The danger for this type is identification with their own righteousness, that is, failing to understand the perspective of those they oppose. All creatures are motivated by self-preservation, and idealists may be seen as a threat to the power and authority of their bosses. The idealist may allow his/her own suppressed anger to leak out by "getting" the boss—for example, publicly and pointedly exposing the contradictions and inconsistencies in a policy. If the idealist does not allow a face-saving way out for a boss, s/he may find that the conflict rapidly escalates to a struggle for survival. When pushed to an "us or them" level, it is reasonable to expect that all parties to the conflict will struggle vigorously, if not violently. This does not mean that idealists are responsible for areas in which they have no power, only for understanding their role in the conflict and for considering how the situation might be transformed into one of mutual advantage.

There is insufficient research to identify the antecedents of this type of character organization. Clinically we have noticed that many of the idealists we have worked with are first or only children. Often they are high achievers who have had success as a result of persistence, single-mindedness, and independence—the very factors that can entangle them in some workplace scapegoating situations.

There is a subtype of the idealist that deserves further mention. This is the gadfly. This sort of person actively seeks out conflict with authority. There is some research showing that a small percentage of victims of bullying are provocative and aggressive themselves.[2] As children they are characterized by an overreactive and poorly regulated emotional response to insult or aggression. They are seen as restless, irritable, and hot-tempered. Prospective studies of their family backgrounds suggest that they experience more punitive, hostile, and abusive family treatment than either nonvictim bullies or nonaggressive victims. Descriptions of these children sound very much like those adults described as "impulsive subordinates" in the organizational development literature.[3] These employees are "problems" because of their provocative challenges to the existing organizational authorities.

The Redeemer

This version of the scapegoat looks very much like the idealist. The redeemer also acts on principle, speaks unpopular views, and is willing to suffer personal loss to protect principles. However, the principle that is being protected by this type is *the maintenance of the organization.*

The primary loyalty is to the system itself, not to a principle extrinsic to the system. The redeemer is deeply connected to the values of the organization and committed to its survival, even at great personal cost. We have seen examples of this type primarily in employees of nonprofit or public-interest organizations and in the helping professions (such as social work, psychiatry, or health care).

This type will work long (unpaid) hours, take on the most difficult projects, and, ultimately, accept the blame for shortcomings in the system. The redeemer truly serves the function of expiation in an organization, and in this way comes the closest to the original, biblical definition of the scapegoat. We believe that this type performs many of the workplace functions that organizational specialists call "the toxic handler."[4] By taking on "impossible" and unwanted tasks, and by serving as the focus of blame and failure, they sacrifice themselves for the "good" of the organization. This allows even very dysfunctional systems to continue to operate. Some overly conscientious managers fill the redeemer role.

This form of scapegoat is sometimes also called the "codependent" employee. By subordinating their own wishes and desires to those of the organization, these employees become "shock-absorbers" for stresses in the workplace. When the pressure to work harder comes, they do. When the workload becomes "impossible," they rise to the occasion, even at the expense of their own health and emotional well-being. Then, when the load becomes truly impossible, they become easy targets for blame. They allow the system to ignore the actual consequences of policies and business decisions by personally taking on the pain that these policies produce.[5]

The cost to the redeemer is obvious. The danger here is misplaced loyalty. Redeemers defend their organizations with the same intensity as they would defend their families. We have found two questions helpful when working with this type: "Is this job really worth dying for?" and, "Who asked you to fix this company?"

The literature in family therapy includes many references to this pattern, which is sometimes called "The Christ."[6] This role often falls to children in highly conflicted families. By attracting attention and blame to their behavior, these children divert catastrophic conflict between their parents. This allows the family to remain "intact"—at least at one level, and so spares the child the terror of the disintegration of the only known support system. The child experiences it as a matter of survival, and if we imagine ourselves in the child's position, we can agree. If we take a wider perspective, however, it is easier to see alternatives—such as living with only one of the parents, a sympathetic relative, or even in a foster home. Part of the task of working organizationally with a redeemer type is to help him/her take a wider perspective and to envision alternatives.

The Fall Guy (or Gal)

While fall guys may appear at first glance to be simply in the wrong place at the wrong time, we believe there are behavioral factors that help identify this type. There is often a period of testing as potential scapegoats are being identified. If targets do not resist this initial probing, their chances of being scapegoated increase. Particularly shy or timid employees (like Sally in the previous chapter) are especially vulnerable. Introversion per se does not lead to being targeted, but rather the response that the target makes to overtures. If the target retreats, becomes flustered, or in some other fashion demonstrates him/herself to be an "easy" target, the process is likely to continue. This process provides some short-term benefit to the organization, as it preserves the existing organization. However, it does so at the expense of examining what are the real causes of the organization's problems.

Again, there is not enough research to describe the antecedents of this type reliably. It would be fascinating to know, for example, whether the "passive victims" of childhood bullying are more likely to be targeted in the workplace as adults. This would require longitudinal studies following chronically bullied children into adulthood, and these studies are expensive and difficult to do. Our clinical experience certainly suggests that there is a connection, as clients who come to us for "job stress" often present with long histories of being abused by others.

Some of our clients, however, come with long and successful work histories, and complaints that things were fine until a new and irrational supervisor took over. They have become the fall guy with no apparent previous history of victimization, and this adds an additional sense of outrage and shame to their experience of being "singled out" for bad treatment. That is, they have always seen themselves as successful employees and members of the team, so their current stigmatization challenges their basic view of themselves. Sometimes in the course of consultation, we are able to discover together some aspect of their personality that may be "setting off" the supervisor, but in most instances we believe that this subtype of scapegoating has more to do with institutional factors (including those that permit destructive and disordered managers) than the target's personal style.[7]

The Organizational Shadow

This is the largest and most studied of the subtypes. The term "shadow" is used by psychologists to describe aspects of the self or society that are submerged, undervalued, or unacceptable.[8] All of us have these qualities. In Jungian theory, not all aspects of the shadow are even what most of us might consider "bad," just different from our usual and preferred ways of being.

When this occurs at a societal level, however, the results are almost always ugly and tragic. Some aspect of the collective that is unacknowledged is projected out onto another group and is attacked. This is seen in the process of the formation of an "enemy," who are first dehumanized, paving the way for murderous treatment that is justified by their supposedly "base" nature. The message is that the enemy is not like us, we are not like them. Collective scapegoating is also seen in the stereotyping of immigrants or racial minorities and in the devaluing of the feminine in our own society.[9] When this happens in the workplace, the target is usually an individual rather than a class or group, though the same principles apply to both situations: the target is selected because of his/her embodiment of some characteristic that the blaming group wishes to disown.

An interesting variant of this occurs in hospitals. There is a conflict in the cultures of physicians and nurses. Most physicians entered their careers as medical scientists, whereas many nurses were motivated by the desire to be emotional and physical caregivers.[10] In the language of Jungian psychological types, most scientists/physicians rely on thinking, sensation, or judgment to make decisions, whereas nurses embody feeling, intuition, and perception. These last three are often associated with the feminine and are devalued as ways of knowing in the medical world. Most nurses are female, and despite some recent progress, the contribution of women in the workplace is still undervalued and undercompensated. Nurses have huge responsibility but limited power in the health care delivery system. The combination of unequal power and differing motivations make nurses prime candidates to be scapegoated, and they frequently are.[11] We illustrate this with the story of Carla, whom we will follow in subsequent chapters.

At forty-two, Carla was a veteran nurse. She had worked as an LVN at the local Veterans-Administration hospital for almost eleven years. Most of that time was on a medical/surgical unit. She liked her work, but tended to keep to herself. Just recently she broke up with her boyfriend. She felt like she needed a change, so when an opening came up on the dialysis unit, she transferred.

At first she was welcomed. The work was demanding and the patient load high. All of her patients were desperately ill. Sometimes they had extreme reactions to their treatment, becoming irrational, and occasionally even psychotic. The families were worried and sometimes very argumentative. The physicians were hard to contact, their orders occasionally confusing and illegible, and they blamed the staff when one of their patients "went sour" (got much worse or died). Carla felt caught between the patients and their families and the physicians. But she told herself, I'm a nurse—what's new? I can handle it.

She noticed that when she went home she felt pretty lonely, and that she was more likely to go to the refrigerator and pour herself an extra glass or two of wine. A part of her wondered about that, but she quickly shrugged it off—she didn't have a problem, she wasn't drinking half of what her mom used to. The unit was short staffed, so when the charge nurse asked her to work some double shifts, she agreed. She was needed, and besides, it beat going back to her cold and dark apartment. After working a double, she was too tired to go to the gym. It was all she could do to open a can of soup, a bottle of wine, and plunk down in front of the TV. She was always on time to work though, and her uniform was always freshly washed and ironed.

So it came as a big surprise to her when the charge nurse called her into her office. She had just received a memo from administration complaining about the morbidity and mortality figures for the unit. The charge nurse pointed out that the number of patients experiencing complications had gone up about a month after Carla started working on the unit. Carla was shocked. She looked at the figures and noticed that the upsurge in problems coincided with the absence of several staff (vacations and sick leave), a marked increase in patients (and so a lower staff to patient ratio), and with the retirement of a veteran physician and replacement by a new, less experienced physician. She pointed this out to the charge nurse who became visibly angry and insisted that the most likely explanation was that Carla was trying to avoid her responsibility and that she had better shape up.

Carla was shaken. She stayed after her shift reviewing her records. Maybe she had somehow missed something. The thought sickened her. No matter what else was going on (or not going on) in her life, she

*prided herself on her work. Her records seemed pretty much in order,
though she did notice how brief and rushed her notes appeared. She
began to lose her confidence. She was afraid to mention her conversation with the charge nurse to any of her coworkers. Besides, she didn't
really know them all that well anyway. She thought about transferring
back to her old unit, but her position had already been filled. She knew
that she would need a letter of recommendation from her charge nurse.
The likelihood of that seemed small.*

*Since the meeting, the charge nurse made a point of checking Carla's
notes. Sometimes she would come out to the nurse's station and make
a point of reviewing them in full view of the ward clerk and the other
nurses, jotting down her own notes in a manila folder with Carla's
name typed on the front. Carla began to fear her. She felt exhausted
from the scrutiny. When one of the other nurses called in sick, the charge
nurse asked for a volunteer to take a double shift. No one volunteered.
The charge nurse looked at Carla. Carla said that she was pretty tired.
The charge nurse reddened and accused Carla of compromising the
integrity of the unit and endangering patient care. Carla reluctantly
agreed. That night, one critically ill patient died, and another became
so disoriented and agitated that he had to be placed in restraints. In
the process, he suffered bruises, which due to his medical condition appeared as dramatic welts.*

*Carla went home in a daze of fatigue. When she returned to work,
she was met by the charge nurse and a hospital administrator. The
family of the bruised patient was suing the hospital, and Carla was
being placed on suspension until further notice. Carla felt as though
she had been punched.*

There are several variations of shadow-scapegoating in the workplace. Targets may be identified by visible signs of difference (their
skin color or foreign accent), their manner of dress (overly formal,
overly casual, poorly fitting, etc.), or their behavior (overly friendly,
aloof, etc.). Sometimes the scapegoat is the department "character,"
a person whom everyone sees as eccentric. This person serves as a
convenient target for humor and for blame, and may personify some
traits that are feared by the rest of the staff, who may regard him/
her with a mixture of pity and contempt. Often this person serves the
function mentioned in chapter 5 of being an object lesson of what can
happen to you if you break the rules or become too nonconformist.
Usually this person is not in immediate jeopardy of further banishment, since s/he is already fairly isolated.

Sam worked as a social worker in a mental health clinic. He did not fit the usual appearance of a therapist. He wore garish suits, loud ties, and gaudy jewelry. He drank heavily and smoked cigarettes like a chimney. He had a series of failed marriages and relationships, and made sexually suggestive comments to the female staff. His conversation to colleagues seemed more concerned with financial matters than with therapeutic technique. Some of his former patients who came back to the clinic politely requested assignment to a different therapist. While by and large staff treated each other with courtesy and professional respect, privately they joked about Sam. He was everyone's nightmare of what they might become—burnt out, disillusioned, alcoholic, lonely, and barely socially appropriate. These projections made it hard to see that for some patients, particularly people who were themselves quite marginalized, Sam was actually a good therapist. It also made it more difficult to confront the effects of clinic policy changes on their own professional identities. That is, it was easier to focus on Sam's perceived relational shortcomings than on the devaluing of relationship that was occurring institutionally.

Paradoxically, a person can also become marked as a shadow-carrier by being too "good." This is another side of the redeemer. Employees who sacrifice themselves for the company not only elicit the envious resentment of their coworkers, but also may eventually arouse the suspicion of their managers. In this case, doubts about your own productivity or adequacy are projected out onto the target who is seen as having "something to hide." When some deficiency is eventually exposed (as is inevitable for all fallible human beings), it is jumped on. Management can use this process to accelerate "competition" between employees and to keep them divided and distracted.

Another variation of the shadow-carrier is in more danger. This is the problem employee who is singled out because s/he personifies some aspect of the managers or the system that cannot be acknowledged. An example of this was Physician A in chapter 5. He attempted to continue to provide care in the fashion in which he had been trained. The organization demanded more "productivity" but officially maintained that the quality of care was not affected by their policy changes. Physician A's behavior highlighted this conflict, so one way to cope organizationally was to attack his ability and competence. Had the organization been willing to acknowledge the effect on quality of their speeding up on quantity, they could have openly disciplined an employee like Physician A for failure to keep up. That is, they could have officially acknowledged that quantity was more important than quality. Since they did not wish to recognize this themselves, their blaming of him was more disguised, though equally effective in isolating him.

The value of the shadow, in organizations as well as individuals, is that s/he represents untapped or unexplored abilities, ideas, and resources. The shadow contains aspects that are disavowed, overlooked, and denied access to the conscious process of decision making. Bringing them back to the table, even as unwelcome guests, adds important dimensions and richness to the decisions that are reached. That is, more facets of the situation can be incorporated into the decision, and a wider range of possible choices can be considered.

The Underdog/Top Dog

There can be no underdog without a top dog. In fact, this subtype most clearly illustrates the degree to which relational templates (see chapter 4) operate in scapegoating. All large organizations have some chain of authority, usually graphically represented by an organizational chart. This chart details the hierarchy of authority, power, and responsibility for making decisions and accomplishing tasks. Often, though, organizational charts do not take into account the informal "pecking order" or hierarchies within work groups and offices.

For example, the positions of receptionist and secretary may be listed in parallel under the clerical staff manager, but in fact, one of the secretaries may actually serve as an impromptu supervisor to resolve disputes between the receptionists. Similarly, there may be implicit hierarchies based on seniority, perceived competence, and personal popularity. What is important for our discussion is the way in which these hierarchies can operate to target some employees as undesirable or "bad," obscuring larger problems in the organization of the workplace.

Jill had worked as a receptionist for the same company for twenty years. In that time she had seen many changes in the pace and procedures of work and in the wages and benefits. She was not alone among the staff in her dissatisfaction, but she was the most likely to express it to others, sometimes even to the customers. Some of the other receptionists privately admired her candor. Others felt very uncomfortable around her. When the manager counseled her about expressing dissatisfaction in front of customers, she was able to alter her "public" behavior, but became more bitter in her comments when neither customers nor managers were present.

The receptionists became divided over how much support to give Jill, though almost all disliked the way the manager had handled the matter. Some felt that the manager "had it in" for Jill and that Jill was being treated unfairly because of her criticism of some of the secretaries, whom she felt were not feeling the same "speedup" as the receptionists. The division of clerical staff into pro- and anti-Jill factions increased, and office morale fell.

Some systemic problems become personalized around one employee. When the issue becomes one of power, with a polarity between "strong" and "weak," many other issues become subsumed and unavailable for examination. In the case of Jill, the division of labor between secretaries and receptionists (particularly around who would answer the phones), the increased pace of work while trying to maintain the same quality of service, and the decreases in real wages and benefits were not addressed. Instead the focus became who had the authority to tell whom what to do. Management felt justified in dealing with "insubordination," and so did not have to deal with the root causes of dissatisfaction. The employees also became distracted by what they felt were abuses of power and were similarly distracted from the origins. Jill became stigmatized and in danger of full-fledged scapegoat status as her manager and those in the "anti-Jill" factor were quick to notice any problems in her work performance. Jill felt herself very much the "underdog."

The strength of the underdog position paradoxically is to expose differentials in power, particularly abuses of power. When you operate from an underdog/top dog relational template, you are exquisitely sensitive to power relations. This strength quickly becomes a weakness, however, if you ignore the fact that as an underdog you may actually give away your power and "inflate" the power of the top dog. By falling into a belief that you are powerless to oppose oppression, you cede the field to the top dog by retreating into sullen silence or sniping. This both emboldens and infuriates the top dog, and the battle is joined around who has the power, rather than on the issue of job performance.

This is a relational template that is present in all of us, and at different times we may play different roles. We must not ignore real differences in the power assigned by our socialization. That is, some of us enjoy privilege that is not earned by our actions but that comes merely from membership in a particular social class, gender, or race.

We may inadvertently amplify these differences by identifying with one pole or the other of this relational template.

When we feel the pull of this template, that is, when we feel that our "authority is being challenged" or when we feel that someone is "pulling rank" needlessly, we need to examine the situation carefully. Are we overreacting based on previous unpleasant experiences? Does this boss or subordinate remind us of someone from our past? Or of some disfavored aspect of ourselves? Checking with trusted coworkers or friends can help separate "old business" from the situation at hand. You may find that you are slipping into an old relational pattern and would fare better if you declined to fill your assigned (and familiar) role. This means that you have to come up with a different way of acting, which can be challenging, but can also allow you to escape scapegoating.

SUMMARY

All subtypes of scapegoating share a common career path—identification, blaming, and banishment. The actual form of scapegoating may vary, and in most cases of scapegoating, there is a mixture of types, as well as a mixture of systemic functions (expiation, intimidation, and distraction). Still, identifying types of scapegoats can be helpful: the idealist (and a variant, the gadfly), the redeemer, the fall guy (or gal), the shadow, and the underdog. Each of the types has qualities that can be useful for an organization, and each strength can also be a weakness, both for the organization and for the individual. Being aware of how an individual comes to his or her "career" as a scapegoat provides ideas for avoiding this role.

To understand this it is helpful to take a detailed look at how the process of identification and blaming happen in the workplace, and we examine this next.

CHAPTER 7

How Are Scapegoats Born?

IDENTIFICATION OF THE SCAPEGOAT

Scapegoating can occur to new employees and to veterans alike. We have already discussed how stress in a system increases the likelihood of scapegoating. So times of organizational change, austerity, or uncertainty are occasions for particular vigilance. Because there are different paths to scapegoating, it is important to assess each situation carefully. This assessment involves looking both at the "internal" (employee) and "external" (organizational) factors that are operating in any given workplace. The first stage of scapegoating is identification, that is, locating and targeting an individual who will carry the blame for the organization's problems. Let's examine some of the ways this can happen.

Auditioning for the Role

Imagine your first day on your new job: you are shown your desk, the lunchroom, and the office layout. Throughout the day people drop by and introduce themselves, or perhaps you are presented to the staff at a meeting. Even though we are adults, it is a little like being the new kid in elementary school. We are being "sized-up" by our peers and our managers just as we are trying to measure them as well. Most of us try to be friendly, to find common ground with our coworkers, and to learn what it takes to "fit" in this environment. We intuitively understand that work occurs in a social context, and that to be successful we need to pay attention to the implicit social rules of the workplace. Usually this works, but sometimes it goes wrong and we become marginalized and targeted. How does this happen? What are some of the early warning signs that this is occurring?

Volunteering for the Role

In chapter 4 we looked at some of the research on bullying. One aspect of this is that kids who have been bullied a lot seem to have adopted the role of victim. Even though some studies suggest that by age twenty-three most of us have left this role behind,[1] we can still see echoes of it in the way that some workers approach their jobs. They seem to *expect* that they will be singled out, and may subtly volunteer for it. It is as though they feel that being misused is inevitable, and by triggering bad behavior, they gain some sense of control. Psychologists call this masochism. It can present itself in a variety of ways. Sometimes it means being passive, timid, or even submissive.

> *Linda worked in a high-pressure office. Her boss had a reputation for yelling at the secretaries. She knew that her boss was under a lot of pressure from his boss to increase "productivity" in the office. So she was already nervous when he called her into his office and told her that he needed a report prepared by 4:00 P.M. that day. She shuffled nervously and her shoulders slumped as he talked, for she knew that the job would take longer than that to do. He must have noticed her posture, because he snapped, "Aren't you capable? We can't afford any dead wood around here!" She blanched, which only seemed to encourage him. His voice became louder as he said, "When the going gets tough, the tough get going. I suggest that you get to work—that is if you expect to keep working here."*

Persons who are naturally introverted are sometimes mistakenly seen as weak. The secretary Sally, from chapter 5, is a good example. Had she been a little less accommodating initially (by politely declining to be drawn in to her supervisor's discussion of her personal life), she might have subtly encouraged her supervisor to "pick on someone else." Sometimes though, employers actually look to hire people that they can pick on.

Hiring the Predisposed

It may serve a scapegoating culture to actually *recruit* a scapegoat. Persons who are depressed, highly anxious, or suffering from attention deficit disorder begin their employment as natural targets. Why would a company hire someone if they expected them to fail? There are many possible motives. Sometimes the applicant has qualifications that lead the company to overlook potential weaknesses, and sometimes there is such pressure to fill a position that employers are not very choosy. But sometimes, whether this is conscious or submerged in the company culture, it is because the "position" of scapegoat is temporarily vacant. We have found that persons who are depressed or who have learning disabilities or attention deficit disorder are often "recruited" for the role of scapegoat.

> *Ivan came to his job interview in a suit that appeared several sizes too large. He said that he had recently lost quite a bit of weight. He acknowledged a tendency to become depressed, but said, "When I get depressed, I work harder." The departmental head insisted on hiring Ivan despite misgivings expressed by the hiring committee. In fact, Ivan did not seem happy, though he did seem to throw himself into his work. Ivan spent a lot of time in his office and made few friends in the department, even though many tried to make him feel welcome. Others experienced him as cool, aloof, or depressingly dependent. So he had few allies when the department head changed his mind and decided that Ivan "wasn't working out." Ivan was encouraged to look elsewhere and left after working only about ten months. Interestingly, his departure was never openly discussed, though many whispered rumors circulated.*

One of the "functions" that Ivan served in this office was to underscore the power of the department head. While the "official" version of reality was that the hiring committee was empowered to make decisions about job offers, the actual power to hire and fire lay with the department head. Ivan became a case example of the difference between the overt and the covert "cultures" of this company. The suddenness of Ivan's departure frightened many into silence, and magnified the power of the department head to make the real personnel decisions. Ivan's brief career as scapegoat served as a reminder of the difference between how the office was "supposed to" function, and how it really functioned.

INVITATIONS TO THE ROLE

If you recall our discussion of interpersonal templates (chapter 4), you will remember that every dance starts with an "invitation." The invitations to the scapegoat/persecutor dance can come in a number of forms: boundary violations, sarcasm, outright hostility, and blame. Each challenge has many possible responses. Some of these responses encourage further scapegoating, and others discourage it.

Boundary Violations: "Excuse Me, but You're Standing on My Foot"

When psychologists talk about "boundaries," they mean the way that we differentiate self from other, and internal (private) experience from external (public). If you are a parent, think about the pride that you felt when your child took her/his first steps, or how much you "hurt" when s/he cried getting an injection. When we are highly identified with someone, we may act as though our feelings are his/hers and vice versa. This can become a problem if it leads to the expectation that both persons necessarily share the same view.

When sociologists talk about boundaries, they usually mean the rules that govern social behavior in a given context. For instance, it might be fine to show up at the company picnic wearing cut-off blue jeans, but not to a meeting with your manager. We will use both meanings of the word "boundaries" as we look at how boundaries are "tested." Part of the natural process of creating a relationship is getting to know where the boundaries are. It is not unusual, then, to have boundaries "tested" as you settle in to a new position. But whether you are new or established in a position, some boundary tests are like "screen tests" for the role of the scapegoat.

If the system is already coping with stress and difference by means of scapegoating, the reactions of an employee to tests in the form of boundary violations allow more precise "targeting" of scapegoats. This targeting can be conscious or unconsciously done, but short of true institutional reform and conscious rejection of the process of scapegoating, the best strategy an employee can have to counter the process is *to recognize it very early*. Blocking early attempts to identify you as a target may not stop the organization from scapegoating, but it may keep *you* from being the victim.

Boundary violations come in a wide variety of forms. All share the common feature of subtle intrusions into areas of your life that are not written in the job description. Here are some common ones:

1. Being asked to work late, work more, or work outside your job description. The culture of some jobs (e.g., an Internet start-up company or a law firm) is that you will stay late until the job is done. But

most jobs set some limits on this. If you see that the limits are not uniformly applied, and that as the "new" employee you are always given extra work, or asked to mail packages "on your way home," or to cover a job for which you have not been trained, be careful. While your employer may be testing your versatility and commitment to the company, he or she may also be checking out how far you can be pushed. If you are a "pushover," you may also be at risk for being blamed and scapegoated.

2. Being given low-status or gender-stereotyped tasks. Some women have come up with creative rejoinders for these occasions. If the boss turns to a woman manager at a meeting and assumes that she will take the "minutes" of the meeting, she might say, "I'll be happy to do it today, but why don't we rotate the position of secretary?" Low-status tasks can also be balanced against one another: "I'll make the coffee today if you'll go to the copy machine and make copies of the report for everyone."

3. Being asked to do your job with grossly unequal resources, staff, facilities, or materials. While it may be reasonable to expect the smallest office or the least desirable cubicle, if your desk is in the hallway or broom closet, watch out. If you are given an unrealistic deadline for a project, it is better to mention this early, rather than the day before the project is due. If you are told to complete a task but are denied essential materials, it is better to explain why the materials are essential as soon as you discover the problem. This runs the risk of being seen as a "complainer," but this may be preferable to being seen as incompetent or unreliable.

4. Being given insincere (or at least premature) flattery. We all like to be appreciated. However, if your manager is gushing with praise before you have truly accomplished much, it may be a sign that he or she has unrealistic expectations. The flip side of praise is always blame. Being singled out for one suggests that you may soon be singled out for the other.

5. Being asked to do personal favors. Mailing personal letters, choosing a gift for your boss's spouse, giving advice on wardrobe, or giving the boss a lift to pick up his or her car are all examples. They may be innocent and harmless acts of kindness, or they may be taken as invitations to expand the boss's reliance on your kindness. Apply two tests. First, does it feel okay? That is, do you feel any discomfort or lingering resentment before or after doing the favor? If the hairs on the back of your neck stand up, look again. Second, does this lead to an escalation? Does your boss ask more often, or ask new favors that feel less appropriate? If the answer is yes, find a polite way to decline or make yourself unavailable to be asked.

6. Being asked about your personal life. Again, this may be due to innocent curiosity, social ineptitude, or a desire to seem friendly. Apply the
same tests as above. If need be, look for ways to decline politely while
helping the boss "save face." You might say, "Thank you for your concern, but I like to keep my business and personal life separate." Then
change the subject back to the business task at hand.

Humor at Your Expense: Laughing at or Laughing With

Humor is a sign that strong feelings exist about a topic. If humor
is directed at a person, it becomes sarcasm, and it is a warning that
the joker has strong feelings about the person who is the butt of the
joke.

Humor can also be used as a tool to deflect injurious intent. That
is, we can use humor to lessen, or even reverse, the social consequences
of barbed comments. Being able to laugh at one's own foibles is both
a gift and an acquired skill. It is a "meta-comment"—a comment *about*
the comment. In effect it can say, "I am big/confident/capable
enough to acknowledge and be amused by my mistake." This helps
diffuse and "de-fuse" the social awkwardness of being laughed about.

If someone in your office is continuing to make fun of you publicly, try to understand why. If s/he seems to enjoy the discomfort of
others, you may need to let that person know you don't intend to be
an easy target (see the next section). If humor is just a way of coping
with discomfort or insecurity about the job, you might try to form
an alliance. If you don't feel comfortable doing that publicly, you
might try speaking to the individual privately. Say something like, "I
can see that you enjoy a good joke—I do, too—but I'm feeling picked
on by you, and I don't appreciate it." If that isn't sufficient to stop
the behavior, you may need to involve your manager.

If it is your manager who is doing this, remind him/her politely
that everyone works better when they feel valued and comfortable.
It is the manager's job to create a workplace that is not a hostile environment. The words "hostile environment" are legal buzzwords that
come from antiharassment legislation, and most managers now know
them.

Mean People Mean Business

Some coworkers and managers are cruel. They enjoy watching
others squirm. If this reminds you of the research on bullying, it is

not accidental. These people are likely to be grown-up bullies. Like the schoolyard bullies, their behavior should not go unchallenged. If you "go along to get along," you may find yourself on the receiving end of an escalating stream of abuse. The most effective cure for bullying is to have allies who make it clear that the bullying will not be tolerated. You must also be willing to stick up for yourself. Be specific about your complaint and clear about the consequences. For example, "George, when you told the entire staff at this morning's meeting that I had been responsible for losing the Jones account, you misrepresented the facts. If you ever do that again, I will not even discuss it with you. I will take it straight to upper management."

Workplace Games: Pin the Blame on the Scapegoat

When a workplace deals with difficulties by shifting blame, it will tend to consolidate the blame by placing all of it on one individual— the scapegoat. Whether the scapegoat is the "new guy" or a veteran, the process is similar. Management may use scapegoating to appease higher-ups (expiation), to intimidate their workers (control), or to direct attention away from their own responsibility (distraction). Managers may scapegoat directly, or they may create a climate where employees do the scapegoating themselves. Since we all have a tendency to scapegoat, it may not take much to pit employees against each other—sometimes this may even be done unconsciously.

Susan worked in a telephone call center. It was a very busy place, with a number of operators clustered in small cubicles. Their calls were randomly monitored by their supervisor. They had to deal with anxious and often dissatisfied customers. They were allowed only a brief time for each caller, and a computer kept track of how long they spent with each customer. Turnover was high and morale low. Jane sat in the cubicle next to Susan. Jane was having a very bad day. She had a series of extremely angry customers; she had had a fight with her husband the previous night; and she felt that her supervisor had made an error on her time card that would cost Jane some money. Jane started yelling at her supervisor, who got up and left the room. While Jane was arguing with the supervisor, Susan tried to pretend that she was invisible.

When the supervisor left, Susan tried to reassure Jane that everything would be all right. Jane yelled that Susan couldn't understand what she was going through, and demanded why hadn't she helped. Susan was terrified. She began to stutter. Jane became even angrier, and stood up, looming over Susan. Susan feared for her safety and slumped over her desk, with her arms over her head, certain that she was about to be hit. Fortunately, Jane turned on her heel and stomped out of the building.

This incident was created by the interaction of a number of factors: Jane's poor impulse control, Susan's fearful reaction (which subtly emboldened Jane's expression of rage), and most important, the supervisor's failure to manage the workplace. First, the supervisor should not have had her argument with Jane while Susan attempted to work in between them—this already involved Susan in the conflict and invited making her a target. Second, the supervisor, knowing that Jane was furious, should not have left Susan and Jane alone in the room. It was easier for the supervisor to get up and leave than to deal with Jane's escalating anger. That left Susan as a target of convenience, and because of her timidity, she was an easier target than the supervisor. Without consciously intending it, the supervisor had promoted Susan as a scapegoat—a target for displaced blame and anger. This can happen quickly or over time, and it may be employees, not managers, who initiate the process. We look at examples of this in the next section.

Swimming with the Penguins

We've all seen nature films of adorable-looking penguins waddling down the ice floe to the water's edge, and then milling about, rocking from one webbed foot to the other, jostling each other in what appears to be a cute "dance." This dance, however, has a more serious purpose. The penguins are hungry and need to fish, but none wants to be the first in the water. This is because none knows if there is a predator—a sea lion or killer whale—lurking in the dark water below. The penguins are caught in what psychologists call an *approach-avoidance conflict*: The first penguins into the water stand the best chance of catching their dinner, but also the best chance of becoming someone else's dinner. So the penguins jostle each other until one of them tumbles in. They all pause a moment. If the water does not erupt in a thrashing red cloud of penguin parts, the entire flock dives in. One of the flock, inadvertently, has quite literally "tested the water" for the rest.

Something similar occurs in the workplace. We call this process *cueing the scapegoat*. Coworkers will promote a scapegoat to test the departmental waters. That is, when a new policy or procedure is being proposed, or a potentially controversial subject is raised, the scape-goat may be jostled into responding first. This "invitation" may be direct—"Jack, what do you think of this plan?" Or it may be more subtle—all eyes turn toward Jack. There may be attempts to "prime" the scapegoat before a meeting—"Jack, I've heard that management is going to make us attend meetings at our lunchtime, can you imag-ine that?" Or to inflame emotions—coworkers look at Jack and roll their eyes or sigh quietly as the boss talks about the need for working lunches. All of these invite the scapegoat to question the new policy and to gauge the reaction of management.

It is important to be aware of whether you have fallen into the role of being "first in the water." If you are always the first to speak dis-sent, look again. Have you become labeled as the department mal-content? If so, you are well into the role of scapegoat, and chances are that management has learned to discount your input. It may be more effective to consciously rotate the role of dissenter. This can be done by telling coworkers who are "priming" you that you hear that they are concerned, and you think it would be great if management heard different voices expressing their opinions. You may wish to ac-knowledge that you are aware of your habitual role. Using the example above, you might say, "Wow, they want us to work through lunch— I'm sure you can imagine my reaction to that proposal, and I'm sure that management can too. What reaction have you gotten from oth-ers that you've told?[2] You know, the more different people speak up about this, the more likely the big guys are to rethink it."

Develop some strategies to help you manage your own behavior in meetings. These may include resolving *not* to be the first to speak and enforcing this if necessary by counting silently to ten (or a hundred if need be!) before responding to a general invitation for "input." It may mean consciously lending nonverbal support (rapt attention and gaze, head nodding, mumbled agreement, etc.) to others who are speaking. If you find yourself getting agitated or anxious during the meeting, become aware of your breathing and allow it to deepen. It can also be very calming to place both feet flat on the floor and to concentrate on the sensations that you feel—the contact between your feet and your stockings, between your stockings and your shoes, be-tween your shoes and the floor.

If you are consistently ahead of the group, you risk being identified and isolated.[3] This is not an endorsement of conformity or "group-think," but rather an observation about how workplace cultures actually operate. Sometimes it is necessary to work behind the scenes to develop sufficient group support to make dissent effective. Family therapists have long pointed out that a system is remarkably resistant to change that originates from only one member.[4] Intervening simultaneously from at least two directions seems to be necessary for lasting movement. These directions can include different people, different levels of the organization, and sources both within and without the organization. What is important for scapegoats to remember is that effective action requires some allies. Since the process of scapegoating involves isolating the scapegoat, it can be difficult to recruit allies. But connecting with others not only combats the group dynamic of scapegoating but also reduces the shame that contributes greatly to the pain of the scapegoated individual.

Enlisting others may mean out-waiting them. If you can consciously cope with your anxiety, you may find that others will speak the message that you have been delivering. They may also then sample the beginnings of the scapegoat role. If they directly experience rejection or isolation from management or the group, they are more likely to be willing to ally with others against the process.

Some workers deliberately plan their behavior in meetings, agreeing beforehand on the order in which people will speak to raise different points and pledging to support each other in case of attack.

Passing the Impossible Test

This phenomenon was nicely popularized some years ago by the "The Kobayashi Maru" episode in the TV series *Star Trek*. As part of a command training exercise, cadets at the Star Fleet Academy are put in a flight simulator and given a scenario that involves mechanical problems and hostile attack. They have to deal with the rapidly escalating crises, knowing that graduation depends upon their composure and decision making under stress. What they don't know is that this is an impossible situation. That is, that every possible response that they make simply leads to more disaster, until their ship is "destroyed" and all hands (including themselves) are "killed." The *real* test is how individuals behave when their attempts at solution fail.

Some organizations deliberately set new employees into similarly impossible situations, partly in the hope that a new perspective may lead to a new solution, but also as a way of gauging the employee's persistence, demeanor, and behavior under stress. A few examples may help illustrate this.

Old Feuds in New Bottles

In this scenario, a middle manager might be asked to create a work group that includes employees who have a long history of hostility toward each other. Or a new employee may be sent as a departmental representative to another department that has had an adversarial or competitive relation with the employee's parent department. In another variant, an employee may be asked to develop a service plan without knowledge that three previous attempts by staff have all been rejected by upper management. Here's one of our favorite examples.

> *Joe was new to the department and was told by his boss that he needed someone to head up a committee to improve staff morale. Joe obligingly agreed and began an earnest survey of the staff to explore what their concerns were, mindful of the fact that because of organizational and budgetary turmoil, any actual changes that he might recommend would probably have to be small and have little impact on the budget. He was delighted to find that a frequent theme in his inquiries was the desire to have a refrigerator in the staff lunchroom. With a little investigation, he found out that, in fact, there was a spare refrigerator in one of the company storerooms.*
>
> *Thinking that he had found the perfect way to please both the staff (who wanted a refrigerator) and the boss (who could get one for nothing), Joe made his report to management. It was rejected angrily. What no one had mentioned to him was that the issue of the refrigerator had been a departmental sore spot for years. There used to be a refrigerator in the staff lunchroom, but it had been removed by management because the staff had not kept it clean. The staff felt that that responsibility belonged to the housekeeping staff. The housekeeping staff felt it was not in their job description and refused. In frustration, management had the engineering department remove it to the storeroom where Joe found it.*

Vetting for Character

Organizations have a legitimate interest in knowing how employees will react to challenging work situations. Often they can gather this information by job history, previous references, or performance on an interview, especially "stress-interviews"—where the prospective employee is deliberately challenged, interrupted, or otherwise stressed. Sometimes employers will purposely make a change to observe the employee's response. An interesting example comes from the *Harvard*

Business Review. A department manager was also serving as assistant general manager, and his name appeared in both positions on the company's organizational chart. He was sent away for a management course and returned to find that his boss had issued a new organizational chart, this one with a blank space for the assistant general manager. Afraid of seeming pushy or insecure, he did not approach his boss about this omission. When he returned from his annual vacation, however, he found that another manager had been given the position and was now listed as assistant general manager on the chart. He had failed an unspoken test—he had not demonstrated sufficient ambition or assertiveness. Worse yet, he began to be seen as an easy target. The boss became openly critical of the operations of his department, and more closely limited his authority and range of projects. Seeing the writing on the wall, the target began to look elsewhere for employment.[5]

Surfacing the Culture of the Organization

The best defense against scapegoating is to recognize it before it happens to you. Is there a history of scapegoating in your organization? Has there been a lot of turnover? Why? If possible, see if you can speak with the person who left the job that you are considering taking. Notice how your coworkers are treated. Do they seem afraid or cowed? Observe how tasks and resources are assigned. Are some workers especially favored and others snubbed? Are the expectations for productivity roughly the same for everyone at the same job classification? Answering these questions will begin to give you a picture of the "culture" of your workplace. Cultures that include favoritism and focusing blame are likely to foster scapegoating.

While you are at the questioning process, ask yourself some tough questions as well. We'll explore the answers to these in the next chapters. These questions will help you assess your personal vulnerability to slipping into the role of the scapegoat:

Does the scapegoat role feel familiar? Have you felt yourself in situations at work, school, or home where you were bullied, harassed, or scapegoated more than others around you?

Do people frequently blame you for things that aren't your fault?

Do people "make mountains out of molehills" when blaming you for things?

Do you feel like you are being made an example of as a way to keep others in line?

Do you feel like you have a "special role" in your workplace, to say what others are afraid to say, and then being punished for it?

Are you seen as a potential or suspected whistle-blower by others?

Do you feel "set up to take the fall" for the mistakes of others?

Do you walk around with a chip on your shoulder, expecting to be picked on?

Do you tend to be a loner at work?

Do coworkers or supervisors make joking or critical comments about your work clothes, work habits, personal mannerisms or habits, religious beliefs, or physical characteristics?

Are you seen by coworkers or bosses as "different" from the others you work with?

Do you violate important unspoken workplace rules or taboos, either on purpose or by accident?

Do you take stands on issues at work based on your strongly held beliefs or principles, and "let the chips fall where they may" without first considering the office politics?

Do you take strong, controversial stands at work that might make you a target, without first talking to trusted coworkers?

Do you look down on the people at work, and not respect, like, or trust them?

Do you try to fix things at work before others even agree they are broken?

Do you dread going to work—feel like you don't know what to expect from your coworkers or boss?

Do you feel like others are always testing you for weakness?

Do you feel like others are talking about you behind your back?

Do you feel like you are walking around with a target on your back?

Do coworkers avoid you, or leave you out of social events?

Are you being asked to do things others are not asked to do—such as work late, do the dirty work, take the assignments no one else wants, and yet you feel that you cannot complain?

Do you ignore or minimize indications from others that you may not be as competent at some areas of your work as you think you are?

Do coworkers see getting at you as a way to get at others or take out on you anger they are feeling toward others whom they may be afraid of or to whom they are unable to direct their anger?

Are you seen as teacher's pet at your workplace? Are you seen as favored, fairly or unfairly, by your supervisor?

Do you feel like you have been hired or asked to do an impossible task but can't say so?

If you answered "yes" to many of these questions, the odds are that you are already well established in a career as the office scapegoat. In the next two chapters, we look at how to begin to step out of the role and take the bull's-eye off your back.

CHAPTER 8

Ditching the Bull's-Eye: Recognizing That You Are Being Scapegoated

No one wants to believe that he or she is doing a poor job. Nobody wants to be blamed for the mistakes of others or for the inadequate organization of the company. One way of coping with unpleasant feelings is denial, pretending that nothing is really wrong, or that everything will work itself out. When you are in denial, you are more likely to ignore warning signs that things are not going well. As the indications of trouble increase, so does your fear. Fear may cause you to *freeze*, like a deer in the headlights of an oncoming truck, and fail to take evasive action.[1] Survival depends on being able to break this "trance" of denial and to notice that you must begin to respond.

The feeling that you are being scapegoated may develop as slowly as a vague sense of increasing isolation, disapproval, and that *something is just not right.* Or it can come crashing down in the form of a reprimand from the manager, a negative performance evaluation, a demotion, or a firing. However it comes, when others are telling you that you are wrong or "bad," it is natural to feel overwhelmed by self-doubt. There may be a tendency to retreat and further isolate yourself. This is as maladaptive as the deer *freezing* on the road. It is crucial to enlist the help of others to begin to assess what is going on both with you and your workplace. A trusted coworker, a knowledgeable friend, a spouse or partner, or a professional can all be resources. The assessment process involves asking yourself tough questions, but it is also an opportunity to learn—about yourself and about others.

OBJECTS IN THE MIRROR ARE CLOSER THAN THEY APPEAR

The assessment process begins with a close look at yourself—what Alcoholics Anonymous has called *A Fearless Inventory*.[2] Ask yourself the following questions:

1. *Is the criticism justified?* This should be rephrased as "To what extent is the criticism of my performance justified?" Identify the things that you have done well and the things that need improvement. Be specific. Come up with a list. Compare your list with the assessment of your critics and, if possible, with a list made by a trusted coworker. If you can't find anything that you've done that could be improved, look again. Some recent research has found that people who are unable to do a job are often unable to identify the skills necessary to do the job correctly, and so they don't notice that they are not performing.[3] If you believe that there is no room for improvement in your work, can you support this? If you can take a differentiated view of your performance, you are already beginning to break down the all-or-nothing framework that characterizes scapegoating. Assuming that you can find both things that you have been doing well and things that you could improve, go on to the next questions.

2. *Who's got the itch? Why now?* That is, who is complaining about you and what else is going on in your workplace? Remember that scapegoating often occurs in times of organizational flux or stress. Are there rumors of change? Talk of financial problems in the company? Is your boss's position in jeopardy? Is your department going to be reorganized? You may not be able to influence the larger picture, but you can use this information to become aware of the forces within the system that may be conducive to scapegoating. This may help you to locate natural allies to resist scapegoating or to understand your difficulties in a larger context.

3. *How do you invite scapegoating?* This is a complex question and may best be addressed by asking yourself a number of related questions. First, what is your impact on others? How are you perceived in group meetings? By individuals? Your impact will depend a lot on the behavior of others and the context in which it is seen. Do even your friends find you a little *prickly? Critical? Out of the loop? Passive? Fearful?* Notice the ways in which you are seen as "different." This doesn't mean you have done anything wrong, only that these are potential openings to separate and isolate you from your coworkers. Specific personality features may also interact with the scapegoater's person-

ality to invite completion of the relational templates that we discussed in chapter 4. For example, the boss's tendency to bully may actually be elicited and encouraged by the presence of a timid and fearful employee.

4. *Next, what do you do that makes it easy to target you?* Are you the lone voice of dissent? Are you the only one who does *not* speak when feedback is requested? Do you call attention to yourself? Do you enjoy "puncturing" the boss's pretensions? Do you react to the boss as though he or she were an important person in your past? Are you creating opportunities for others to criticize you?

Look again at the types of scapegoats we discussed in chapter 6. Are there ways in which your situation resembles any of these? Actual scapegoating situations often involve some combination of "types," but does one type seem more like you than others? If so, you may want to pay special attention to the advice for each type that is at the end of this chapter.

Remember: Scapegoating is a particular type of relational template. It is a "dance" done between a targeted individual and others in the context of a group. Recognizing how you go along with the dance gives you more chances to choose *not* to continue the dance. Knowing how the powerful pulls that you feel are rooted in your own history makes it easier to decide not to repeat patterns just because they are familiar. Let's look again at Sally, the secretary we met earlier in chapter 5.

Sally's parents had divorced when she was quite young. She had little contact with her dad but was a dutiful and attentive daughter to her mother. She was a very "good" little girl. Still she could not shake the lingering feeling that something must have been wrong with her for her father to leave. Like many children, she found it easier to contend with the pain of loss by blaming herself. If she was at fault, at least that meant that something could have prevented her father from leaving. She tended to accept blame readily, even when it wasn't fully deserved.

As an adult she had a very uneven work record. She was extremely successful working with some bosses, and very unsuccessful with others. She began to notice a pattern: She seemed to have more difficulties with female managers. She would take on extra projects to please them, would stay late or come in early, and would often find the boss treating her as a confidante about her personal matters. At some point the boss would switch from being a "pal" to being critical. Sally would become flustered and make more mistakes. She would try to compensate by working harder and by making effusive apologies. Instead of appeasing the boss, this would only intensify the criticism. Sally would become agitated, anxious, and eventually she would slip into a serious depression. This pattern was repeated several times over the course of twenty years.

Sally decided that she could not afford to keep repeating her pattern and became curious about how it actually happened. With the help of a therapist, she began to explore both her love for and her rage at her parents. She had not allowed herself to feel either anger or disappointment at her dad for leaving, and had instead become scrupulous in her caretaking of her mom. At the same time, she herself longed to be taken care of.

Sally came to see how she was inadvertently reenacting a family drama at work. She saw how she would subordinate her needs to what she thought her boss needed and how she secretly resented this. She began to see how she created unrealistic expectations about her work performance and her ability to "make things right" for her boss. When Sally's resentment would begin to "leak"—either by not being around to "soothe" her boss or by making an error—the boss would turn on Sally, and she would be thrown back into a state of longing and loss that she had known, but suppressed, as a child.

Notice that Sally's problem mostly occurred with bosses who were "narcissistic"—they needed a great deal of emotional support from their employees. This style of relating is very prone to sudden shifts: you can go from being best buddy to archenemy very quickly.

To fully understand how you "invite" scapegoating, you need to become aware of your own motives, actions, and feelings. This can be a difficult but worthwhile process. It not only involves the ability and willingness to look "inside" yourself, but also requires exploring the opinion and reactions of trusted others. One way of locating your geographic position is to take "readings" from several different observers and the "triangulate" or point at which they all agree. Note that your true location is best determined when you have several different points of reference. The same is true of your "interpersonal" position.

The key to getting accurate information is communicating a willingness to hear it. If you find that you have a tendency to dismiss or overreact to coworkers' comments about you, you may be training them to avoid talking to you frankly. Nobody likes to be criticized, teased, or laughed at. One way to cope with the discomfort of criticism is to cultivate an attitude of curiosity—temporarily set aside your fear or irritation and wonder what is going on. For example, you might respond to an implicit criticism by asking calmly and with *genuine* interest, "What did I say that made you say that?" If you can be genuinely nondefensive and curious, you are showing the other person that you are open to hearing what s/he is thinking. You may find it useful to repeat or rephrase what you hear, and reflect it back: "So it feels to you like I'm not pulling my share of the load."

It's hard for you to believe that you could bring scapegoating on yourself. But if you can show others that you are willing to hear from them about what you are doing that is turning them off, you are already reducing the isolation that fosters scapegoating. Remember: Connection to community creates "allies" in the struggle against scapegoating.

If you have generally felt successful in social and work functions, look to friends, coworkers, and perhaps employee assistance specialists for your "triangulating" feedback. If you have had lifelong patterns of difficulty in relations with others, both in your social and work life, you may need to explore these in a professional therapeutic relationship.

5. *What am I bringing to this problem?* Think about your last three jobs. Jot them down on a piece of paper. Get a mental picture of the boss at each. For each job ask yourself, "What did I dislike about my boss?" and write that down. Do you see any pattern or similarity in your answers?

Is there any similarity to what is going on now? Does the boss's behavior remind you of any aspects of your own behavior that you don't like? Is it possible that you did something that triggered the boss into behaving that way? Does your relation with the boss remind you of your relation with anyone else in your life? All these questions point to the power of projection—how we subtly re-create familiar patterns and especially how we attribute our own disowned thoughts and feelings to others. We'll say more about this process later in the chapter, but beginning to uncover your own projections is a necessary part of the "fearless inventory."

THINKING OUTSIDE THE BOX

There is an old Cantonese saying: "If you don't change your direction, you will wind up where you are headed." Scapegoating is a peculiar problem for most of us because the things that we might usually do to cope with criticism—work harder, protest our innocence, or become indignant—actually often make the situation worse. When we work harder, it is taken as proof that we were slacking—"See, he could have been working harder." When we protest our innocence, the question of our "guilt" is raised in the community. And if we become indignant, it is seen as further evidence that we "don't fit in."

Successfully coping with scapegoating requires a more strategic approach. Being strategic means having some idea of where you want to go and what you want to happen. Think about your goals. Is it more important to you that the system change or that they stop picking on you? What is your overriding concern? Is it to keep this job until you get another? Is it to have your boss apologize? To have your coworkers support you? What would have to happen for this to occur? Is there any way that you can promote the change that you want?

This may be an unfamiliar way to think. You may resist the idea of having to "manage" your managers. After all, you are being paid to do the work, and they are being paid to "manage" the workplace. Still, when the organization of the workplace is conducive to scapegoating, you have only a few choices: suffer, leave, or try to outmaneuver the system.

Systems are generally able to absorb the input of any one member without changing. After all, feedback from one member can always be discounted or ignored. The key to promoting organizational change is to intervene at two or more levels simultaneously. For example, consider approaching a critical manager to discuss his/her concerns directly, while *also* enlisting the aid of a sympathetic supervisor or a group of like-minded coworkers for a wider discussion of organizational problems in the workplace. Make sure that the initiative for this appears to come from someone other than you.

If you are already entrenched in the role of scapegoat, it is essential that you are not the only person who brings these problems to managerial awareness. As a scapegoat, much of what you say can and will be discounted. Protest, or at least opposition to scapegoating, needs to come from several sources; otherwise, the system will "absorb" it or see it simply as "whining."[4] As appropriate as it is to oppose bad behavior, it is important to do it strategically. We explore more strategies in the next chapter. Let's continue to focus on how to recognize the ways you might be participating in scapegoating.

"I'D LOVE TO DANCE BUT I'M SPOKEN FOR, AND BESIDES, I DON'T DO THE MAMBO"

There are many subtle ways that we are invited or thrust into the role of scapegoat. Sometimes we can only begin to notice the pattern over time. Sometimes it is our reaction to an overture that determines whether we will become a scapegoat or whether someone else will be picked.

We looked at some of the "invitations" in the last chapter. How do you know when you are playing along? First, examine the flow of an interaction. Replay it in your mind. Who said what? What happened next? Most important, did your feelings change as the interaction progressed? Did the other person show any changes in his/her feelings? Did the feelings feel proportional to what actually happened, or did they seem somehow "larger than life"? It is this larger than life feeling that clues you in to the fact that something else is amplifying the exchange. This something else can be the activation of an old relational template, or it could be projection. Projection is the attribution of feelings or thoughts from the accuser to the accused. The accuser then attacks these, even though they originated with the accuser.

> Sally's boss, Jane, was working against a deadline to get financing for a project. It was a large project, and Jane was having trouble keeping track of the details. Jane prided herself on her organizational skills and found it very difficult to acknowledge that she had mislaid some important documents. Instead she became increasingly critical of Sally, jumping on any mistake. Sally had helped Jane look for the documents. Sally had thoroughly searched the office and her own desk for the papers, all to no avail. Jane insisted that she had given Sally the papers, even though Sally knew this was not so. The next morning Jane confronted Sally, waving the missing papers, which she said she had found on Sally's desk. She immediately stripped Sally of her regular duties and relegated her to filing.
>
> Sally did not know if another worker in the office had found the papers and placed them on her desk (no one would admit to doing this), or whether Jane had found the papers in her own office but was too embarrassed to admit it. What Sally was certain of was that the papers had not been on her desk the previous day.

Sally was already in the role of the scapegoat at the time of this incident, so it was very difficult for her to protest her innocence. Her solicitous attempts to help Jane find the papers only fueled Jane's embarrassment that they were missing. Sally's "helpfulness" was reframed as incompetence—obviously she hadn't found them, Jane did. Jane could not tolerate the possibility that she had made an error—it did not fit with her picture of herself. Furthermore, the papers were important, and Jane was rightly very worried about what would happen if they were not found. The unacceptable idea—*I have made a very big mistake*—became *You have made a very big mistake*, and so the emotional "balance" of the office was temporarily restored. Jane felt vindicated and once again "in charge."

Dealing with Projections

If you are the object of another's projections, you must first become aware of the situation. Sometimes it is clear that what you are being accused of is outrageous, untrue, and more characteristic of the accuser than of yourself. When this happens, you can deal with it this way: *you can join, expand, and interpret.* If accused of being X, you can say—*I agree with you that X is pretty undesirable here* (joining). *Maybe we could look at how X tends to happen throughout the office* (expanding). *Perhaps there's something that promotes X in all our meetings* (interpreting).

When you *join* with your accuser, you line up on the same side of the issue—that X is an undesirable thing. You not only don't resist the attack, but you also take the attacker's point of view. You try to understand where the attacks are coming from and show your willingness to discuss the points of agreement that you share. Often attackers are expecting you to resist their statement of the problem, and they have prepared a series of points to bolster their position. What they are not prepared for is agreement, and this "unbalances" them temporarily. It is as if they were leaning hard to push open a sticky door that suddenly swings open on freshly oiled hinges.[5]

When you *expand*, you take the accuser's point and elaborate it. This helps to create a broader focus. It identifies X as the problem, not *you* as the problem. In that sense it both diffuses and redirects the conversation. You not only *agree*, you also *offer other instances*, showing that you really understand your accuser's concerns. If the accuser contests this, s/he is undercutting the validity of his/her stated concern and exposing the malicious intent of the criticism. Expanding on your accuser's point further helps your credibility to recontextualize or interpret.

Interpreting may involve providing a different explanation—*Maybe X is happening because everyone is worried about the possibility of lay-offs*—or it may be an invitation to look for one—*Why is X happening at so many of our meetings?* It is important to avoid name calling—*It's because you are a lousy boss who has to blame others to save his own reputation*—but it may be necessary to invite the accuser to reclaim or "own" his/her projections—*Maybe you see X in others because you sometimes feel like doing it, too.*

If a projection feels especially harmful and inaccurate, you may need to confront it directly—*I hear you saying that I am the primary person whom you see as doing X, but I disagree and, in fact, I think I am being singled out for blame for a larger problem.* This can be done in a polite and businesslike tone, but you are making it clear that not only is X a problem, but also that the *process* of projection and externalizing blame is an even bigger problem.

Confrontation, of course, carries risks: of being fired for insubordination, of being labeled a troublemaker (but note that you are already being labeled), or of making the authority figure angry. But the alternative is to allow a severely inaccurate view to go unchallenged, and your lack of dissent to be taken as admission of the accuracy of the accusation. You have to weigh the pros and cons in each situation. While you may intensely dislike direct conflict, you may feel worse about yourself if you remain silent.

Expand Your Repertoire of Responses

Although it is true that *anyone* can be targeted as a scapegoat, some people are more vulnerable than others. If this is not your first experience in the scapegoat role, it is an especially important opportunity to discover how you got there and what else you might do. One interesting way to accomplish this is to write your own story, that is, to write a brief history of your experiences at work. If nothing else, this will help you get your chronology straight if you decide to register a formal protest.

The purpose of this exercise is much more than documentation. Include how and when you began to feel that you were being isolated, blamed, and excluded. Put in as many facts as you can—who said what to whom and when—but also write how you felt. Pay attention to changes in your sensations, perceptions, and thoughts. For example, when did it start to get hard to get up in the morning to go to work?

When did you begin to feel uneasy around your boss or your co-workers? What was that like?

Now write a *happy ending* to the story. Imagine how things might change at work so that you could feel good again, or perhaps how you could get a better job. Reread what you have written. What has to be different in order to make this happen? Psychotherapists have long used techniques like "journaling" to enlist clients' emotional expressiveness, creativity, imagination, and problem-solving abilities. Now researchers are beginning to document the effectiveness of this type of work.[6]

Putting your story down on paper allows you some emotional distance. In that way you may be better able to see possibilities than when you're caught up in the heat of the moment. It is important not to ignore your own contributions to a problem. Mistakes offer valuable lessons for what to do differently next time. Despite feeling battered or bruised, it is also helpful to note that you have survived a difficult experience. Writing a happy ending can alert you to strategies you haven't considered and may alter your emotions enough to enable you to change the social reality of your situation.

SPECIAL QUESTIONS AND ADVICE FOR SUBTYPES

Although the following questions have value for all scapegoats in their self-inventory process, we have grouped them by subtype and added some commentary and advice for each. Each subtype represents one pole of a relational template or pattern. In order for it to be fully activated, it has to interact with a workplace environment that promotes and completes the pattern. More than one subtype can be active at a time, so you may recognize yourself in more than one of the groups.

For Idealists

Who asked you to fix this job? Idealists sometimes make themselves available for scapegoating by offering unsolicited advice to their managers. While the advice may be good, it also may be extremely unwelcome. Comments and criticisms can be more effective if they can't be consistently localized in one individual.

How much justice can you afford? Even granted that you are right, the struggle to have the rightness of your position recognized may be very costly. Most whistle-blowers get fired, and only a few ever receive compensation for their troubles. It is important to decide what your goal is, and how much you are willing to sacrifice for it. It may be worth the pain, but that is a decision that is best made consciously.

Are you more interested in effecting change or in being recognized for upholding a principle? One of the key traps for this subtype is righteousness. Because you believe you are taking a principled stand, you assume that others are not. This can lead to a perception that you are arrogant or superior and severely undercuts your ability to recruit allies. This can make it harder to actually produce organizational change.

Can you wait for reinforcements? One of the dangers for the idealist is identification with the archetype of the hero, especially the hero on the solitary quest. By solitary quest we mean the notion that any one person can conquer the system *alone*. It may take a hero to "lead the charge" for change, but if you are the only one who is charging, you have already *isolated yourself* and increased your vulnerability.

Are you counting on "fair play" to carry the day? The world is not fair, and neither is the workplace. Fairness is a social construction—it is a way to envision how the world *ought to be*. But it is not an accurate model of the way the world actually is. If you believe that reason and rules of fairness will prevail in organizations, you are misreading the situation. These rules may apply, but decisions are often reached for very different reasons. To be successful, you need to pay attention to the way things are, as well as to how you wish them to be.

For Redeemers

Do you believe that your sacrifice will transform this job? It may, but it may be just as likely that you will simply be replaced like a worn-out part on a machine. Despite the cost of recruiting and training a replacement for you (which may be in the thousands of dollars), most companies treat their employees as if they were disposable. While you have unique abilities and qualities as a human being, it is rare that these will be recognized in the workplace.

How long can you keep it up? Redeemers can be the heroes in an organization, keeping it functioning even in times of chaos or demoralization. If the chaos continues, the redeemer can become exhausted, depleted, and burnt-out. When times return to normal, they may be an embarrassing reminder of the costs of that period, and hence a candidate for scapegoating.

Is this job really worth dying for? The effects of prolonged stress are well documented in the aggregate.[7] We have known for a long time that, on average, stressful events increase the likelihood of serious illness, accidents, and death. We are just beginning to be able to study the physiology of the individual in enough detail to document changes in immune system functioning. This allows us to make a clearer connection between stress and disease in individuals. We don't yet have a way to quantify the degree of stress, but we have some interesting results from research with animals that point to the perception of helplessness (inefficacy) as a major stressor.[8]

Although all occupations entail some risk, it is worth exploring how much risk you are accepting by taking on the organizational problems of your workplace.

For Fall-Guys/Gals

Do you think your competence makes you immune? There is an old joke that even paranoids have enemies. Even excellent workers can be singled out. When the motive for scapegoating is intimidation, it may be even more effective to "make an example" of a competent worker in order to instill fear in others.

The only effective defense against deliberately manipulative scapegoating is to enlist allies. This can be very hard for professionals who pride themselves both on their competence and on their independence. Often they choose to leave a company rather than to oppose scapegoating. When this option is blocked, they seem especially vulnerable to demoralization. An alternative is to ally with others to combat the process. The very fact of reaching out to others reduces the shame and isolation that they feel and begins to restore some sense of dignity and effectiveness.

When you were little, were you a frequent target for bullies? It is unlikely that any of us escaped childhood without being bullied. If you were bullied frequently or consistently, some vestige of that experience may remain. This may cause you to be either especially sensitive to bullying behavior at work or to be especially in denial if it occurs. Either pole can create problems. The best protection against automatically repeating a pattern is awareness that the pattern exists. Examining your own history can help you decide how much work you need to put into overcoming your earlier experience.

For Shadow-Carriers

What is making you feel that there is a problem? Begin with your feelings. Are the hairs on the back of your neck beginning to stand up? Often we have information that we register emotionally before we understand it consciously. Become aware of your own reactions to others. Are you feeling fearful? Irritated? Especially bored? Have these feelings been growing gradually, or have they suddenly intensified? Have you changed or has your workplace? Or, more likely, how has your relation to your workplace changed?

Are you getting feedback that you don't belong? Are you feeling isolated or that you are "different" in some unacceptable way? Notice the behavior of others at work. Do you find people avoiding you? Do conversations stop when you enter a room? Do people look at you out of the corners of their eyes?

Identification as "different" and isolation from the group are danger signs for scapegoating. The essence of the shadow-carrier is that s/he represents some aspect of the group that is unacceptable to the consciousness of the group and that is being projected onto the scapegoat and attacked. This process is by definition unconscious, so the antidote is to increase consciousness. This process may be resisted vigorously, since the group does not wish to acknowledge the projection. But once you have identified for yourself what the projected attribute is, you are in a much better position to find openings to comment on it.

For Underdogs

Do you frequently feel challenged or oppressed? If so, you may be being drawn into unnecessary power battles that exhaust you and make you a target for projection and blame. In Aikido there is a principle of "noncollision." When your opponent makes a vigorous move at you, you sidestep. This is called "stepping off the line," since you no longer are directly in line with the attacker. But neither have you abandoned your position. Instead you have chosen to step to a spot that maximizes your opportunities and preserves your integrity without meeting force with force. From this position you can turn and "join" your opponent, unbalancing him/her and redirecting the force of the attack into the ground. This takes a great deal of skill and expert timing. But the principle is basic: If you meet force with force, you risk being overpowered if your opponent is stronger than you. If you step off the line, you can direct your attacker's force to its natural, unbalanced conclusion (in Aikido you are "assisting your opponent to the ground").

Consider what opportunities you might have to "step off the line" when you feel an invitation to a power battle.

SUMMARY

Scapegoating is both a systems and an interpersonal problem. It is difficult for victims of scapegoating to acknowledge that they may have contributed to the problem. We have found that it is even harder for people to acknowledge or "own" their contribution to an interpersonal problem without assuming responsibility for the *entire* problem. If you remember that interpersonal problems by definition involve more than one person, it may be easier to examine your role in the problem without falling into "all-or-nothing" thinking.

The process of honest self-assessment is best done with the help of trusted others in your workplace, not just those who will agree with you out of friendship. It is especially important to involve others who know you in the problematic context.[9] You need friends or allies who are "good enough" to be able to disagree with you and still be trusted. If you don't have these kinds of people in your professional life, this in itself is a warning sign of vulnerability. If you are isolated, you are already halfway down the career path of the scapegoat (identification, isolation, and exclusion). Professional consultation should be considered to help sort out the individual and systemic contributions.

If you *do* have friends who will help you in the self-assessment process, then you already have a "ladder" to help you "climb out of the hole." You have both a tool (knowledge) and possible allies to oppose scapegoating. Beware of any reluctance to listen to or use feedback from trusted others.

> Sue poured Carla another cup of coffee and replaced the empty box of Kleenex. Carla's eyes were red from tears, and a pile of wadded-up tissues littered Sue's kitchen table. Carla had only a few friends, but fortunately for her, they were good ones. After hearing Carla out, Sue asked her what she planned to do. Carla had no answers. Sue asked about the nurses' union. Carla said that she had never dealt with it except to complain about the dues that were deducted from her paycheck. Sue suggested that maybe it was time to learn. Sue worked as

an accountant so she also suggested that they take a quick inventory of Carla's assets and liabilities. Sue told her that as far as she could see, Carla had the following assets: she was nice, competent, conscientious, and apolitical. She also had the following liabilities: she was nice, competent, conscientious, and apolitical! For the first time in two days, Carla laughed. Sue pointed out that some job situations are actually set up to convert assets into liabilities, but that Carla had some choices about how she could use her skills in new ways. Sue also gently suggested that Carla's tendency to withdraw when she felt hurt made her a pretty easy target and that she had seemed pretty unhappy even before her trouble at work.

If you have found yourself described in one of these sections, then it is important to enlist your network of friends and/or outside consultants to help you avoid "progressing" to the next level of scapegoat status. The process of avoiding or relinquishing the scapegoat role involves assessing one's own participation in the "dance." When you know *how* you are playing into the role, you have some choice about whether to continue. This may mean that you have to learn some different ways to behave. In the next chapter, we discuss strategies for combating scapegoating.

CHAPTER 9

Machiavelli in the Lunchroom

Although this book aims to help you find out about the dark or shadow side of your organization, it is important to point out that it may not be enough for you to just go to work on time and do your job well. The game of success is not always fair. Sometimes the deck is stacked. Awareness and even some extra effort to cope with workplace "politics" may be necessary to survive and thrive in your organization.

We believe, as our mothers taught us, that honesty is the best policy. Not only does it allow you to preserve your own sense of integrity, but also it is easier because you don't have to remember what story you have told each person. However, there is also a place for tact, discrimination, and occasionally even deception. (For example, see the section later in this chapter on "seeding rumors" to uncover the source of gossips.) If your workplace culture does not value or even punishes honesty, you may want to change companies. But if you stay, you may wish to consider some classic political wisdom.

Niccolo Machiavelli was a late-fifteenth-century Florentine statesman who is famous for writing *The Prince*, a book of advice to a young ruler. The Italian peninsula of the fifteenth and sixteenth centuries was a world of feuding city-states and families with private armies. It was a dangerous place of intrigue, shifting alliances, and treachery. Machiavelli's book described a number of strategies for controlling and manipulating others. His name has become an adjective to describe cynical and brutal tricks of statesmanship. However, in *The Prince*, Machiavelli repeatedly speaks of *virtu*, an Italian word that we can roughly translate as *know-how*. He was much more concerned with the efficacy of his methods than with issues of morality, which he felt was a thin veneer over the desire for power. He summed this up nicely: "[I]t has seemed to me wiser to follow the real truth of the matter rather than what we imagine it to be."[1] While we do not endorse methods that deliberately hurt others, we can agree with Machiavelli that survival may depend on anticipating attack and realizing that attacks can come from many directions.

We wish that we could say that Machiavelli is no longer relevant, especially to the modern workplace. Unfortunately, many of his observations are still quite applicable to the process of learning to swim in the dangerous waters of a scapegoating workplace. We refer to him from time to time in our discussion of how to cope *strategically* with scapegoating.

THINKING STRATEGICALLY

The word "strategic" comes from the ancient Greek word for general (*strategos*), and originally meant planning military campaigns. While there is an old Chinese saying that "life is war," we have come to use the word "strategy" more civilly, to denote advance planning to achieve a goal. Thinking strategically involves at least three major elements:

1. Identifying your goals.
2. Considering before you act whether your action will further your goals.
3. Keeping in mind how others are likely to see or react to your action.

The first element is the easiest. Ask yourself what is most important to you in your career. Is your goal to work here until you can escape to a better job? Is it to try to make the current workplace a place where you can be comfortable for years? To make it fair? To survive? To feel that you are doing your job well? This first element of strategy means always keeping in mind what you want to accomplish. Usually you will not be able to achieve all your goals, so it is crucial that you prioritize them. The strategic actions you take will depend on what you want to achieve.

Jim wanted to attend a workplace-sponsored conference on new computer networking techniques. He had not used his educational leave for the year, so he put in a request to Bill, his supervisor. Bill also wanted to attend, and so he told Jim that they could not both be out of the office at the same time—request denied. Jim bristled at the unfairness of the situation. This was not the first time that Bill had ignored procedure in order to gain personal advantage. Jim was tempted to go over Bill's head to the department manager. Then he reminded himself that Bill was vindictive and that Bill would soon be filling out performance reviews for the yearly "merit" pay increases. Jim decided that he would rather have a chance at a pay increase, and so he graciously accepted Bill's decision.

The second element is to consider *before* you act whether your action will move you closer to your goal or farther away. This is easy to say but often difficult to know. If you answer honestly when the boss asks for feedback on his/her plan, will this help or hinder your goal of getting a raise? If you question a colleague about what seems to you to be his/her marginally ethical business practices, can you do it in a way that furthers rather than hinders your desire to work in a united and ethical office? Ask yourself what information you have about the likely outcome. For instance, in the first example: Does your boss value honesty? Has s/he demonstrated this? Do you have any examples? Is s/he able to take criticism as long as there is also some part of the plan that you praise? Sometimes you can benefit from consultation with trusted colleagues to get answers to these types of questions, but the responsibility for the success of your strategy ultimately rests with you. Machiavelli noted a cautionary principle: *"A prince who is without any wisdom himself, cannot be well advised."*[2]

Often you will not have the luxury of time for such on-the-spot deliberations. This underscores the importance of thinking ahead and of trying to anticipate difficult situations, so that when they occur, you have a response ready that will maximize the chances that you will reach your goal. Especially if you are working in a scapegoating environment, you will have to devote some time to thinking about strategy. This can be done with friends, outside consultants, and on your own. It *is* extra work, and the only pay you will receive is the increased opportunity to reach *your* identified goals.

While it may be difficult to know in advance if your action will move you nearer to or farther from your goal, this may be easier to assess after you have acted. Notice the reaction to your action. File it away for future reference—it's valuable information. Consider the military origin of the word strategy and remember that success (or failure) in a skirmish does not usually predict the outcome of the battle and that even a retreat may be done strategically. Your goals are more long-term, so consider each action in terms of the long haul. Periodically reassess your progress toward your goal. Are there other actions that you could be taking to move toward your goal?

The third element is the most complex and difficult: trying to anticipate how the other (combatant, boss, accuser) will see your action. This involves taking the perspective of the other, whom you may fear, dislike, or distrust. It may be very uncomfortable for you to imagine that in the other's eyes, you look like a whiner or troublemaker. Still it is important to consider this other's interests, perspectives, and likely reaction. Taking the viewpoint of the other does not mean that you must give up your own. Mature empathy involves the ability to hold at least two points of view simultaneously—your emotional reality and another's. Empathy is a crucial aspect of what Daniel Goleman has called "emotional intelligence." In the workplace he has identified an "Emotional Competence Framework" that includes self-awareness, self-regulation, empathy, and social skills.[3] These are basic skills that can greatly reduce your chance of being scapegoated. This is part of what Machiavelli means when he cautions that the prince who is without wisdom himself cannot be well advised.

When you see a situation as though through another's eyes, you get important information that can guide your actions. Imagine that the boss sees you as a rebellious child—just like his "unmanageable" teenager who is making home life miserable. If you can see that, you may feel some compassion for his pain, which then allows you to let go of some of the anger you feel at his autocratic blaming, and so you can respond in a quiet rather than an angry fashion. Considering it likely that he feels very unappreciated by his teenager, it may also suggest that you will be more effective if you speak your appreciation of sections of his plan before offering suggestions for change.

To see through another's eyes is a lot of work and may be a difficult skill to acquire. Try practicing with a friend, but be sure to ask first, since otherwise your behavior may seem strange and a violation of the implicit "rules" of your friendship. Start out by doing some of the "active listening" exercises discussed in chapter 8. Practice reflecting the emotional part of your friend's message, as well as the overt content. For example:

You: "How about going out to that new Thai restaurant?"
Friend: "Hmmm, I don't know, wouldn't you rather have pizza?"
You: "Sounds like you're not too happy with the idea of Thai food tonight."

Invite your friend to let you know if you've "got it right." When you both feel that you are pretty consistently accurate, you can graduate to the next exercise: the empathic understanding of empathic failure.

No one can be empathetically accurate all of the time. When we do not feel understood, it can be pretty painful. For some people it is intolerable, and they react as though they have been deeply insulted. *All* relationships can benefit from some way of coping with failures to understand the viewpoint and feelings of the other. Communicating to the other that we understand that s/he does not feel understood is one way of repairing a relationship that has suffered an (inevitable) empathic failure.[4] The form of this communication usually goes like this: "When I did X, it seemed like I intended Y, and it made you feel/think Z." For example: "When I put you on hold yesterday to check another call, it looked like I was more interested in that other call, and it probably felt like I didn't really value our friendship anymore." This does several things at once—it helps the other person feel understood in his/her pain or anger; it signals your emotional ability to understand; and it says that yours is a relationship where such difficulties can be discussed and possibly overcome.

This takes practice and a genuine willingness to put yourself in the other's emotional shoes, even (and especially) if it puts you in an unfavorable light. If you are not able or willing to do this, then *don't try it*. Half-measures will only do more damage to the relationship. People who are sensitive to emotional rejection are usually extremely good at detecting insincerity or someone who is just "going through the motions." Interestingly, we have found that scapegoating bosses are often such people.

Be very careful not to use empathy sarcastically. If your tone indicates condescension or mockery, you will enrage the other. Remember that reflecting is not the same as parroting. You must truly put yourself in the other's place. Suspend judgment. Cultivate curiosity and compassion. This may be difficult. The first time most people practice this it feels as though they are abandoning their own position. Again remember that mature empathy is not "either/or" but "both/and"—your position *and* the other's.

If you are having trouble keeping sarcasm out of your voice, it is better to walk away until you cool down. Excuse yourself to go to the bathroom, get a cup of water, or ask if you can discuss the situation later. If you can, practice on neutral (but trustworthy) persons. Say, "This is what I want to say to my boss. How does this sound?" Listen to their opinion. If they think you are being sarcastic, believe them. Because this is *social* reality, not "the truth," this is one area where someone else may be a better judge than you of the impact of your words.

If a coworker is embarrassed or has suffered a loss of face, empathy can also be expressed by silence or a change of subject. But be careful not to confuse empathy with pity. Pity actually creates distance— to receive it implies a loss of social status. Most people, especially narcissistic bosses, will experience pity as a condescending attack.

A final consideration about strategically taking your "opponent's" viewpoint: whether you are accurate or not, if you are attempting to see things from another's viewpoint as well as your own, you are more likely to be able to notice information from that person's response to your action. That is, your action will act as a probe for information about the system. Like a reconnaissance patrol, you will be attempting to make sense of any reaction, gauging the position and strength of the forces against you.

In a scapegoating workplace, the immediate threat may be coming from your supervisor, but the larger battle may be a clash between old-line managers and new ones from the head office of the conglomerate that just bought your company. The trouble you are having with your supervisor may be a symptom of the anxiety and uncertainty that is rapidly spreading down the organizational chart. If so, you may want to pick your allies carefully, depending on which side seems the most likely to prevail. Or you may want to distance yourself from both sides.

The key to successful strategy is good preparation. Crucial to preparation is good information. Let's examine some tools for gathering information, again with the guidance of our fifteenth-century *consigliere*, Machiavelli.

Awareness

"For if evils are anticipated they can easily be remedied but if you wait till they come to you the remedy is too late and the sickness is past cure."[5]

One of the most common errors is the belief that "it can't happen to me." You may prefer to believe that if you do your job, are courteous, and dress appropriately, you will be immune from the ravages of office politics. By now, however, you will recognize this belief as another instance of the powerful force of denial. In many job situations this is an adequate solution. There will always be office politics, and in most offices their impact on the "good" employee will be minor. In a scapegoating workplace, however, denial can be extremely dangerous.

While denial spares you the worry and anxiety of seeing that trouble is brewing, and of having to make choices that you would rather not make, it can also allow problems to build up. When the defense of denial fails, you are suddenly confronted with powerful emotions, which may be experienced as overwhelming. This intense rush of feeling actually disorganizes your thinking and makes it even more difficult to cope. The antidote, as Machiavelli suggests, is in recognizing problems early and planning a strategic response.

Assessment

"[M]en in general judge more by the eye than the hand, as all can see but few can feel."[6]

Your best tool is your own power to observe—to see things as they *are*, and not as you wish they would be or fear that they might become. Think about your workplace. Watch how people interact. Is flattery the rule? Is everyone treated with courtesy? Who jokes with whom? How are disagreements handled? Do managers rely on blame to get things done?

Note particularly how managers and employees respond to limits. For instance, how did the manager react when one of the secretaries politely told him that she couldn't type the report that he just handed her until she had finished the departmental timecards? What emotions seemed present? Did the manager take the job to someone else? How did that person respond?

No one instance is likely to be definitive. Look for patterns. Think about the office as a system. When we think about systems, we think more in terms of roles than personalities.[7] Roles in this context are like roles in a theatrical play: They describe the interaction and relationships between the different characters in the drama. The dynamics of the system are like the plot: They control the overall course of the action. In order to change the outcome of the drama, the plot has to be changed. It is no wonder that many scapegoats feel like they are helpless players in a tragedy—in some sense they are characters in a play that they did not write. Instead they are adding their own interpretation of an ancient role. There are two solutions possible: change the script, or try to get yourself "recast" out of the role of scapegoat.

Changing the organization's script can be very difficult for any individual (see chapter 11 for a fuller discussion of this), but with awareness it may be easier to "play" your way out of the scapegoat's part. One way to learn more about the "script" is to pay attention to the history of the drama.

Using History

"I have been able to find nothing in what I possess which I hold more dear or in greater esteem than the knowledge of the actions of great men which has come to me through a long experience of present-day affairs and continual study of ancient times."[8]

Roles can be filled by different people, but the roles remain. This means that the history of a workplace can be a guide to uncovering the roles that are part of the organization's "culture."[9] Always ask yourself, has this problem or issue come up before? Using the analogy of a drama, think about whether this "play" has been performed before. How was it handled in the past? Are there any similarities? Are there any "old-timers" who can give you a perspective on what has happened before? Are they reluctant to talk to you? Do different people see things differently, or is a pattern beginning to emerge?

History is the story that people make up about what happened in the past. It is an arrangement of various "facts" in some edited and prioritized fashion. It is also an attempt at explanation of how things got to be the way they are now and often a justification for the current situation. Remember: The story that is made up also tells us something about the author. History is usually written by the "victors," and tends to support their viewpoint.[10] When you are gathering "history" from different people, remember that the story also tells about the values and viewpoint of the source. If you get very different stories, or if people are reluctant to discuss an event, you have probably surfaced an important aspect of the organizational culture. That is, you have discovered some event about which people feel strongly and have different perspectives. Often these strong differences indicate that some "official" version of events is being invoked. This may be as close as you can get to a peek at the script. This may help you understand the motives behind the official version. When you understand the motives of the characters, you can provide a better "performance."

As a nation, Americans are remarkably optimistic. We tend to disregard the past in favor of looking forward to a better future. Sometimes this blinds us to seeing repetitive patterns that lurk under the official version of the present. Pausing to look back, taking an historical perspective can reveal obstacles and make our future planning more realistic.

For example, if you learn that the last two persons who had your job "didn't work out," you might realistically wonder why. Listen carefully to the "whys." If the official story is that they didn't perform their jobs but the office gossip is that the new manager was under fire for the department not meeting its quotas, you can be pretty sure that you are in danger of being the new scapegoat. If you want to stay, you should probably think about how you could demonstrate your value to the new manager's *manager*. Just in case, you might also consider looking for another job.

Triangulation

"Nevertheless a prince should not be too ready to listen to talebearers nor to act on suspicion, nor should he allow himself to be easily frightened. He should proceed with a mixture of prudence and humanity in such a way as to not be made incautious by overconfidence nor yet intolerable by excessive mistrust."[11]

No one viewpoint is likely to reveal a complete picture. When navigating by the stars, we need to take more than one "fix" on our position.[12] This is called "triangulation." By coordinating readings taken at two different positions, you can get a better idea of where you really are.

As we discussed in chapter 8, it is a good idea to get viewpoints from different people in your workplace. This includes people who may see things *differently* from you. If you don't have colleagues at work whom you trust enough to honestly, though perhaps tactfully, discuss office politics, you are in a very vulnerable position. Without "feedback" you can easily magnify small incidents, personalize the impersonal criticism of your work, or ignore real warning signs. You might see danger where it isn't, call it upon yourself, or blunder into it unawares.

Ted had been a manager in the company for many years. He told the newest supervisor, Janice, that one of their coworkers was "out to get her job." She listened with curiosity and tried to get a full picture of her supposed vulnerabilities and the "plot" to get her job. She also listened for other themes, including Ted's motives in telling her "in confidence." She had heard that Ted thought women too naive to be good managers in their company. She was unsure if he was really describing an employee who wanted to take her job, or if Ted himself felt she was unfit. She also wondered if she was being tested by him to see how she would handle news of a plot against her. She asked questions designed to pull out as much information and opinion as she could get before she reacted.

After meeting with Ted, Janice consulted with trusted coworkers and subordinates to double-check the information Ted had given her, without letting on about the source of her concern. She did find the ambitious coworker, a man named George, and, over a few months, she began to form an alliance with him, rather than act fearful or hostile toward him. She helped him get a promotion to another part of the business.

Notice that Janice resisted her impulse to act quickly and defensively. Instead she gathered the information that she needed to act strategically. Most important, she did not rely on any *single* source of information. She sought the opinions of many, and hence got a truer picture of events.

Even if fellow workers are too frightened to stand up with you in a crisis, they may be vital and crucial sources of information. You may already have such sources, or you may need to cultivate them. Building a well-tuned intelligence network can help you greatly to develop an effective strategy. Governments do this and so can you. Two students of corporate culture, Terrence Deal and Allen Kennedy, have noted: "Spies, storytellers, whisperers, cabals—these people form the hidden hierarchy . . . a lowly junior employee doubles as a highly influential spy."[13]

If you are a generally shy person, it is especially important to develop relationships with your coworkers. Listen with genuine interest. Let them know that you understood what they said. This can be done nonverbally, with nods and murmurs of assent, and by sympathetic reflection—rephrasing their statements in your own words. Let them know about you, too. Generally, as people become more comfortable with each other, they reveal more about themselves. As far as you are comfortable, match the level of intimacy that they offer. If they tell you something about their families, or their personal lives, think of some similar aspect of your life that you are willing to share. If you feel that the others are revealing too much, just listen sympathetically. Most of all listen without offering judgment, especially if they are telling you something about how they see you at work.

Learning who plays important informal roles in the "hidden hierarchy" can give you inside information about the workplace culture that you won't learn about in the official house organ or organizational chart. Developing an effective strategy is a lot easier when you have "the inside scoop" and a real history of your department. The actual reasons that people before you have left, been promoted, or otherwise gotten clear feedback from management and peers can then guide your strategic planning.

Flexibility

"Now since the prince must make use of the characteristics of beasts he should choose those of the fox and the lion, though the lion cannot defend himself against snares and the fox is helpless against wolves. One must be a fox in avoiding traps and a lion in avoiding wolves."[14]

One of the very difficult tasks of combating scapegoating is to know when to oppose it directly—like a lion—and when to operate indirectly—like a fox. Each approach is appropriate to some situations and inappropriate to others. Finding the right "mix" depends on the circumstances and abilities of the "prince." You will have to decide for yourself how to proceed in your situation, but the discussion that follows may help.

Finding Allies

Allies can be found in the workplace as coworkers, sympathetic managers, organizational specialists, and so on, or outside the workplace as labor lawyers, unions, the press, regulatory agencies, and so on. There is strength in numbers, and since the scapegoat role is by definition an isolated one, anything that you can do to ally with others will reduce your isolation.

Allies can be discovered, but they can also be cultivated. We have already discussed the importance of empathy in building relationship. But it is also important to consider how to know that your allies are trustworthy. Most relationships are built up over time, and trustworthiness is also evaluated over time. One way to check is to give your ally some information about you that makes you *slightly* vulnerable, and then watch what s/he does with it. For instance, if you admitted something embarrassing to your ally, did it later come back to you from someone else?

Past performance is an indicator but not a guarantee. If someone has shown loyalty to you in a small matter, s/he may or may not stick up for you in a crisis. However, if that person has never defended you in small matters, it is extremely unlikely that s/he would stand with you in a serious situation. Also consider the stakes for your ally. Is what you are you asking going to endanger his/her position or prestige?

Strong systemic forces will push for your isolation. These include reframing your attempts to ally as signs of your weakness, of being an "agitator," or of attempts to cover or excuse your "responsibility" for the problem.

The "lion" will cope by "naming the game," that is, by pointing out that s/he is being singled out for blame, by directly contesting accusations, and by identifying ploys that transfer blame/responsibility. This can be a very powerful position—especially in opposing scapegoating that is based on characteristics like race or religion, which are legally protected, or when the scapegoater is applying rules in an unfair or selective fashion, contrary to the policies of the wider organization.

The lion may also be effective by force of reason or strength of personality. The advantage of this direct approach is that it can nip scapegoating in the bud, before it has a chance to develop much momentum. The disadvantage is that it openly joins the battle, and it risks the danger of escalation and discipline for "insubordination." It may also create resentments that merely submerge rather than resolve the conflict. The lion should remember that s/he is managing the manager's reaction. The manager must be able to maintain the sense that s/he is the boss. Think strategically—it may not be valuable to win a "battle" if it weakens you too much for the "war."

The "fox" will subvert by deflecting criticisms, always leaving the boss a face-saving "way out," and by working behind the scenes to create allies. The fox will actively assess the power structure of the organization and ingratiate her/himself with people who may be of help. This might mean trying to anticipate the ally's needs or interests and doing projects that match those interests.

This could also include setting out deliberately to make an ally of the person who is doing the scapegoating, especially when that person has some "authority." This can be done by subtly pointing out your value to the scapegoater. If you make the scapegoater "look good," s/he may have more difficulty seeing you in the all-or-nothing "bad" way that characterizes scapegoat thinking. If you make yourself indispensable in some way, the scapegoater may shift to another target. Machiavelli notes: *"Hence a wise prince must adopt a policy which will insure that his citizens always and in all circumstances will have need of his government; then they will always be faithful to him."*[15]

Standard advice to those who want to advance in a company is to "make your boss look good." Hopefully your boss's goals reflect those of the organization, and making her/him look good can be done ethically and without a loss of your self-esteem. Making your boss's top priorities your top priorities will reduce your odds of being scapegoated. If you have a boss whose priorities you cannot ethically or practically carry out, you must honestly assess if you should transfer or quit. Ideally, honest disagreement about how to achieve goals is not only tolerated but also valued. If this is not the case, you may need to look for another job.

Interestingly, the scapegoater may also shift the target to someone else if it appears that you are indebted. By having "done you a favor" and shifted the target, the scapegoater can perhaps convince him/herself that you aren't "all bad"—after all, if you were, why would s/he have done you a favor? Again, Machiavelli has a comment: *"It is in the nature of men to see obligation in the favors they have conferred just as in the benefits they have received."*[16] This ploy—which we call "the-child-in-need-of-protection"—can sometimes slip "under the radar" of a narcissistic boss who feels the power of dispensing favors as reassurance of his/her own importance. This ploy may be most effective in top dog/underdog scapegoating situations. We consider this to be a very risky strategy, however, since the scapegoater can just as easily see you as weak and an easier target.

Both the lion and the fox need to remember that being surrounded is a very weak position—if you can be isolated, you will likely soon be defeated. Allies alter isolation. So can some tactical maneuvering. As much as possible do not take on the scapegoater alone. Instead have the voice of challenge come from a group, a committee, or an outsider. This makes it harder to identify and isolate any one worker as the scapegoat. If a group presentation is not possible, rotate the position of dissenter so that it is harder to pin the label on any one person. Leave room for the scapegoater to retreat while saving face—a cornered opponent can be more dangerous, and, besides, your long-term strategy may involve you all having to work together for a while.

The lion may temper her or his courage with the cunning of the fox. The nerve to confront directly may be tempered by strategy and even compassion for the adversary. For example, a move by the boss to scapegoat can be opposed immediately in a forthright and business-like fashion, and then allowed to drop, providing the boss with a face-saving way out, while sending the message that any future attempts to scapegoat will be opposed as well.

> *Charles received a phone call from an irate customer who demanded immediate action from the head of the department, Mr. Jones. Charles attempted to reach Mr. Jones, but his line did not answer. After several attempts to reach him, Charles left voice- and e-mail messages for Mr. Jones. He also asked the departmental receptionist if she had seen Mr. Jones. The next day Charles received a furious call from Mr. Jones, who said he had been in his office, and why hadn't Charles relayed this important message? Charles politely but firmly indicated that he had tried to phone him, had left messages, had a timed and dated e-mail expressing the urgency of the call, and had even spoken with other members of the department about Mr. Jones's possible whereabouts. Charles then said that he was sorry for the delay, and if Mr. Jones would like, he would contact the client with an appointment time for him to speak directly with Mr. Jones.*

By standing up to Mr. Jones's attempt to shift blame, Charles took the stance of the lion. He made it clear that he was not going to back down, and further that he was willing to involve others to expose Mr. Jones's behavior if necessary. But he also let his "threat" (of exposing the boss) remain implicit, and he played the fox in offering a general apology for the "delay" and in offering to contact the angry client, allowing the boss to retain control and to save face.

Dealing with Rumors and Gossip

People who are being identified as scapegoats are often the objects of gossip and rumor. It can be very frustrating to hear a distorted version of some personal or professional information when it has worked its way around the office and finally gets back to you. It is especially difficult to counter because the source of the rumor is often impossible to trace.

If you do know the source of the rumor, the lion strategy would involve arranging to speak privately with the gossip and to let him/her know, politely but firmly, how destructive rumors are for the organization. You can also let your preference for direct communication be known, your good intentions, and your willingness to hear directly if you have inadvertently given offense. If rumor spreading continues from the same source, that person's malice or inability to control his/her own behavior will be clear. At that point it may be necessary to pursue the intervention of someone higher up in the organization, like a senior manager or the company ombudsperson.

The fox may be creative in detecting the source of rumors. One way to find out the source is to deliberately "seed" some information about yourself with a coworker and observe whether that "information" enters the gossip pool. This is similar to the technique that you can use to learn which of the magazines or charities that you subscribe to are selling your name and address to others. Each time you subscribe use a unique spelling of your name (or a different middle initial). When you receive unsolicited mail, you can deduce the source of the "leak" by the spelling. The "information" you give must be distinct enough to be recognizable when it gets back to you, "attractive" enough to repeat, believable, and unique—that is, you can only tell it to *one* person.

Jim's friend Jill told him that there were rumors going around that he was cheating on his wife with one of the secretaries. Jim was furious and wanted to confront the source of the gossip, but Jill said that she had heard the rumor from several people, and that they would be embarrassed if Jim confronted them. Jim knew that the rumor was untrue, but he also knew that several people in the department who claimed to be his friends enjoyed gossiping, and were more than a little jealous of his position. So Jim took on a project. He found opportunities to casually introduce unique "personal" information into individual "confidential" discussions. For instance he told coworker A about his interest in hang-gliding, and coworker B about playing water polo (both fictitious interests invented for this test). When Jim heard a giggled rumor that he was into "water sports," he suspected that B was the source. He "confided" some more (false) information to B, and when that came back to him as well, Jim was sure. He decided not to confront B, fearing that to do so would only further enrage him and lead to even more destructive rumors. However, he stopped letting B in on private information, and gradually reduced his contact with B.

It might have been most productive for Jim to have told B directly that he knew that B was the origin of the gossip and to have indicated that B was violating company policy and creating a "hostile work environment." This might have led to an apology and some restoration of the relation between Jim and B. However, if the workplace culture implicitly supported gossiping, this would likely have only motivated B to retaliate by escalating the campaign of rumor.

Responding to Attacks

Attacks can come directly, indirectly, in public, or in private. Your response needs to take a number of factors into account:

1. The relative power position of both parties—is the attack from a co-worker, a supervisor, or a boss?
2. The context in which it occurs—at a staff meeting, at your yearly performance evaluation, or at the office Christmas party.
3. Your strategic goal—to secure your performance bonus while secretly looking for another job, to smooth things over for the next few years, to leave with integrity, and so on.

Public attacks are complex. Attacking you in public may further separate you from your fellow employees, making you embarrassed and implicitly warning others not to be too closely associated with you. Or it may demonstrate the scapegoater's own poor control of the situation, thereby weakening his/her position in the eyes of the group. Your response will depend on your confidence, skill, and goals. This is a situation that demands the courage of the lion and the wits of the fox.

Consider your audience. Have they secretly been hoping that someone will stand up to a bullying boss? Are they already so frightened that they live in terror of open conflict? Is there anyone who is likely to speak up to back you up? Who is listening, and who are they likely to tell? Have you done your homework and lined up reliable allies? Will a soft answer be seen as capitulation, appeasement, or a strategic move demonstrating the attacker's irrationality?

Breathe deeply, feel your feet and your hands, and find your own center. Feel the integrity of your own body. Determine a goal for your response: to further your main priority, to maintain your self-respect, or to correct what you feel is inaccurate. Then, and only then, formulate a response. This may mean that you take a little longer than usual to respond, but the wait will make your response more strategic.

You may be able to use humor to counter sarcasm.

Boss: "Well, Jim, we are all so-o-o glad that you finally graced us with your report."

Jim: "Thanks! I hope it will prove the adage, good things are worth waiting for."

You can even make a joke at your own expense.

Boss: "Well, Jim, I hope your report has more substance than your introduction did."

Jim: (smiling) "Me, too!"

Showing that you can make a joke about yourself sends a message *about* the message, namely, that you are a person who is secure enough to laugh at your own expense.

Out-think, don't out-shout or out-muscle your opponent. Your calm may unbalance your attacker. Answer softly, but don't collapse. Be neither defensive nor offensive. Instead, think about where you want to go. Sidestep the attack and move toward your goal. This is the strategy of the fox—but a fox who has spent a lot of time working out with the lions at a martial arts dojo!

Some attacks cannot be sidestepped easily. These may occur in private, particularly around issues such as performance reviews or other critiques of your work. Use the acronym **AABCD** as a template for handling supervisor's critiques. The acronym stands for:

Acknowledge
Ally
Be specific
Check-back plan
Document

Listen to your supervisor's criticism and *acknowledge* it. Feed it back so that you let it be known that you understand his/her complaint. Think about the accuracy of the complaint. Perhaps it is valid and something that you do need to change. Even if you feel that it is not accurate, don't contest it yet. Instead, *ally* with the supervisor by agreeing that you think that behavior could be problematic. Then ask him/her to *be specific* about what behavior is desired. If something is mentioned that you are already doing or have done, only point that out after your supervisor has committed to the view that this is a desirable behavior. That way s/he can't shift the ground, offer a new criticism, or accuse you of sidetracking. Agree on a plan to monitor and evaluate your compliance, and set a time when you will *check back* with each other. Give yourself a reasonable period to demonstrate change, but not so long as to allow a buildup of many other grievances. Finally, write down or otherwise *document* the interaction and the agreements that you have made.

We'll give some examples of how this is done when we return to Carla's story.

Maintaining Boundaries

In chapter 7 we saw how boundary violations could be used to identify likely candidates for scapegoating. Here is where the lion excels in politely but firmly maintaining his/her boundaries. This may involve saying "no thank you" to extra work, longer hours, or other infringements on personal and professional boundaries.

Please take careful note: Many companies have probationary periods in which they may terminate you without cause. You need to consider carefully whether you risk termination by clarifying your role. Then again, a company that would terminate you for polite but firm limit-setting may not be a place where you would be happy working. Weigh the risks and benefits according to your own situation.

The fox knows that there are cultural norms in every workplace situation for how to set boundaries. For instance, in a business that values families, it may be acceptable to decline to stay late because you have a family obligation (an anniversary or a child's "back-to-school" night). In a different workplace culture, these may not be considered valid reasons. Instead, announcing that you have another business engagement (a meeting with a client, etc.) will be taken as a valid excuse.

It is important to understand the norms in your workplace. Notice what seems to be valued by your manager. If you must disappoint your supervisor by not staying late, try not to compound the affront by asserting that your values are more important than his or hers. While it is truly not your manager's business why you need to leave at your regularly scheduled time, you may be faced with either having to give an explanation or having to appear rude. In such circumstances, the fox may plead a previous business appointment even as s/he is heading out the door to a PTA meeting.

When scapegoating is underway, your options may be severely limited, and you may have no other choice but to respond directly.

Carla was surprised by the union's reaction. This was not the first complaint that they had received about the treatment of nurses on Carla's unit. A union steward contacted Carla and immediately contested her suspension. Carla was back at work while her case was being grieved. The charge nurse was clearly furious. The other nurses looked at Carla with a mixture of respect and mistrust. At lunch, one of them approached her and told her that she appreciated someone finally standing up to the administration. Carla thanked her for her support. She began to notice that others on the unit also had questions about how things were run. Later that day the charge nurse came out to the station and made a point of reviewing Carla's notes. She pointedly asked the ward clerk, in Carla's presence, if she had seen Carla actually administer a medicine to a patient, Mr. Jones. Carla politely but firmly intervened and said that of course she had, that she had clearly charted this, and that if the charge nurse had questions, she would appreciate being asked directly.

When the charge nurse, the hospital administrator, Carla, and the union steward sat down to review Carla's case, Carla surprised herself, and everyone else, by first sympathizing with the hospital's concerns about the family's complaint. Carla made it clear that she expected the hospital to share her professional concern for good patient care and that she was sure they could all agree on this point. She proceeded to list a series of procedural changes that she thought could enhance patient care and reduce the chances of similar incidents. Carla won her grievance and her record was cleared. However, none of Carla's suggestions for improving patient care was implemented.

Carla continued to have problems with the charge nurse. She came to realize that the charge nurse herself was caught between the union, the hospital administrators, and her own professional standards. This made it a little easier to respond to the charge nurse's abrupt and sometimes sarcastic directives. Carla began to be assigned to less-desirable shifts, scheduled irregularly. Though Carla had eleven years with the hospital, she found that contract language allowed the charge nurse to assign work not on overall seniority but on the basis of seniority within the unit. She actively began to search for another job. One day the charge nurse instructed her to take a patient down to X-ray, a job usually reserved for an orderly. Carla pointed out that she could not leave the unit while she had other patients to care for. The charge nurse accused her of insubordination and demanded that she comply. Carla bit back her anger and reminded the charge nurse that both had legal and professional responsibilities to their patients and that she was respectfully refusing. As the nurse stormed back into her office, Carla picked up the phone and called the union.

Carla was again written up, and once again won her grievance. It became clear to her that she was going to continue to be targeted. She weighed the benefits of her eleven years of employment: the accrued seniority, vacation, medical insurance, and retirement plan. She weighed the costs: the likelihood of continued conflicts with her supervisor, the emotional tension of trying to change a system that did not seem to listen, her distaste for the "politics" surrounding her job, and the chance that her alcohol use would in fact get out of control. She decided that the costs outweighed the benefits. She went to the charge nurse and obtained a positive, if not entirely heartfelt letter of recommendation. She resigned from the hospital and accepted jobs through a nursing registry while she looked for a more permanent position.

Notice that Carla avoided blaming others. She made strategic decisions based on what she felt was important in her life: her integrity as a nurse, the dangers to her health from drinking and from chronic emotional turmoil, and her desire to make a decent living. She found a way to satisfy her objectives. That the system did not change was unfortunate, but common.

Carla's documentation occurred primarily in her patient charting. She might also have kept notes of meetings she had with the charge nurse, copies of any e-mails or directives she received, and accounts of any incidents relating to the conflict with the charge nurse. These would have involved a description of the situation, a verbatim account ("he said/she said"), and the dates, times, places, and the names of others who were present and who might bear witness.[17] These accounts are most telling if they are completed immediately after the incident (so called "contemporaneous notes"), but if they are complete and accurate, they have value no matter when they are done. Ideally, give a copy of your record of events to a trustworthy party outside your department. Put the record in a sealed envelope and ask them to sign and date the sealed flap of the envelope. This establishes the date of your concerns, so that you can't be accused later of making things up out of "sour grapes."

These notes may be helpful as evidence should the matter ever become a part of a legal proceeding. At the very least they serve the important psychological purpose of giving you something active to do—and thereby counteracting the hopeless feeling that you are a passive victim of circumstances.

Inoculations against Accusations

"Against one enjoying such respect conspiracy is difficult; it is also difficult to attack him if it is generally understood that he is a man of character and respected by his people."[18]

There are some ways to reduce the likelihood that you will be targeted. Obviously, doing your work well is one. But often it is not enough. Scapegoating is so rooted in the unconscious culture of human groups that there is no guarantee that you can avoid it, no matter how perfect or "impeccable" your behavior. Still it is possible to anticipate and "inoculate" yourself against some attacks. As Machiavelli noted, if you are respected by your people (your coworkers), you are a more difficult target.

Earlier in this chapter we discussed recruiting allies. Respect also comes from others seeing and noting your integrity. Carla didn't "mix" much with her coworkers, but when she stood up to the charge nurse's accusations, she won some grudging respect. Imagine how much more effective she might have been had she been talking to her coworkers before the suspension. Sensing a potential issue and making casual "by-the-way" comments in advance alerts others to the situation, makes them potential witnesses, and combats isolation.

There are subtle, and perhaps even unconscious "invitations" to step into the role of scapegoat. You may be indirectly invited to bend or break an office rule.

Anna's off-site meeting was canceled at the last minute, leaving her with a gap in her schedule. She immediately left a voice mail with her manager, Dan, letting him know that she was available for other duties. He phoned her back, thanking her but telling her that he knew she was a conscientious worker, and that she didn't need to notify him of changes in her schedule because he trusted her to find some other productive use of her time. She thanked him for his confidence in her, but remembered what a big deal Dan had made about the time card of another employee, and quietly reminded herself to always notify Dan of her schedule changes.

Dan may have felt sincere in his assessment of Anna's honesty and productivity. But he was also inviting her to break rules (about scheduling) that he had disciplined others for violating. If Anna had accepted his (unwitnessed) invitation, she would have risked isolating herself (as the boss's "favorite"), and left herself vulnerable should

Dan's opinion of her change. By continuing to notify Dan of her schedule changes, she was both following the "letter of the law" in her office and also sending an implicit message to Dan, "Let's keep everything businesslike and both sides protected."[19]

Thinking strategically is foreign to us, and it may feel manipulative or sleazy. Most of us come into our workplace with an attitude of trust. This is a position that we hold in our personal lives that we would like to extend to our workplace. We would like to be able to just concentrate on doing our work. But it is important to recognize that while the workplace *is* a social institution, the rules are different from the rest of our "social" life. We have to be aware and proactive in order to survive, especially in a workplace culture that supports scapegoating.

Self-Care

Whether you act as a lion, a fox, or move between the roles, it is important to realize that thinking strategically may be exhausting. It is more work than we are used to. It is important to set appropriate limits. We can't always be "on duty." Find places where you can be yourself *un*self-consciously. This can be with friends, family, or true community.

Look for ways to recharge outside the toxic system. Physical exercise, meditation, connection to the natural world, and, most of all, fun are all restorative. We explore this more in the next chapter.

In the meanwhile, look for opportunities within the toxic work environment to find some sustenance. These "islands" of sanity may be few and far between (a lunch "outside" with a trusted colleague, a quick but meaningful exchange about a movie you saw, a shared sympathy card for an ill coworker), but they almost always exist if you look for them. Think of them as rocks for crossing the swamp of a scapegoating workplace.

A final reminder from Machiavelli is in order: *"[T]he only good, reliable, and enduring defense is one that comes from yourself and your own valor and ability."*[20]

CHAPTER 10

The Road Back: Recovering from Scapegoating

Scapegoating is such a powerful organizational force that despite their best efforts, decent and competent people are isolated, blamed, and cast out. When this happens, the scapegoated person may experience overwhelming feelings of shame, worthlessness, and a rapid alternation between helpless despair and fantasies of revenge.

Most of us are highly identified with our jobs. When we are getting to know someone, one of the first questions we ask is, What do you do? We often equate what we do for a living with who we are.[1] To lose your job is to lose one of the important aspects of your identity. It is no wonder, then, that scapegoated employees feel shaken to their core. This sense of not knowing who you are is terrifying. But it can also be liberating—it can be an opportunity to examine your values, your direction, and your sense about what really matters.

Because the prospect of losing your job is so painful, you may deny the possibility that you are being targeted. Even though warning signs may have been present, they were ignored in order to avoid feeling apprehension and fear. So when scapegoating culminates in dismissal or demotion, it may be experienced as coming "out of the blue." This surprise increases the emotional shock and adds to the sense of being overwhelmed.

The feeling of being overpowered is an additional shock, especially to people who usually feel more "in charge" of their lives. We have found that scapegoating is particularly painful to middle managers, skilled white-collar workers, and professionals (engineers, nurses, etc.). Facing forces beyond their control challenges some of the ideas that they have about their own ability to control events. For example, Carla took pride in her ability as a nurse, knowing that her patients' very lives depended on her skill, knowledge, and good judgment. Yet she felt powerless, small, and overwhelmed when the charge nurse suspended her.

When other people, particularly people in positions of power, tell you that you are not doing your job, it is natural to feel doubt. Doubt that causes you to examine your own performance critically but fairly can be useful. Doubt that leads to paralysis is not.

FIRST AID FOR SCAPEGOATS

Perhaps the most important advice is to override your desire to slink away and hide. Instead, connect with others. *Tell someone you trust what has happened.* Begin to rally support. This can be extremely difficult to do when you are acutely feeling ashamed and defeated. If you feel you can't do it, maybe one of your friends can help you. If you feel that you have no one, seek professional help immediately. Many companies have employee assistance programs that will provide help even if your employment has just been terminated. Clergy can be a resource. Many communities maintain free telephone crisis-counseling services. There are also many competent counselors and psychotherapists, both in public agencies and in private practice. Recovery is a complex process. Simply finding a new job is not enough. It is important to examine and cope with feelings of loss, rage, and shame. When the feelings are processed, it is possible to think consciously about your relation to the workplace. And then it is possible to be strategic in picking your next job.

Dealing with Loss

It is important to acknowledge that your loss is real. No matter how unpleasant the workplace environment has become, most scapegoats do not leave willingly but are forced out. Even if the scapegoat had powerfully mixed feelings, the experience of being forced to leave adds the sense of powerlessness to the unpleasantness of loss.

Sadness and anger are normal. Grief is an ancient and powerful emotion that seems particularly connected to awareness of our connection to others.[2] We most often think of grief in the context of the death of someone we love, but we can feel grief over the loss of possessions, position, and even at the loss of some idea or view of our *self.* Psychologists group all of these under the concept of "the lost object."

Grief shares many symptoms with depression, but there are some important differences: grief tends to be more acute and connected with thoughts of the lost object or things that were associated with the lost object or situation (favorite songs, smells, places you went together, etc.); depression is more pervasive and chronic—that is, the dark mood is both more persistent and less focused on the lost object. Some people believe that depression also involves a sense of guilt—of having done something wrong or having failed to do something that was necessary.[3] With scapegoating, the sense that the scapegoat contributed to his/her own banishment is a powerful force to direct normal grief into a more pathological state of depression.

The National Institute of Mental Health estimates that more than 9.5 percent of the American population suffered from depression in the year 2000—that's 19 million Americans.[4] Depression is the *leading* cause of disability worldwide among adults; it is second only to heart disease in the economic burden of disease in the industrialized world. Of course, not all depressed employees have been scapegoated, but many scapegoated employees become depressed.

Depression can be a serious problem. It is not only common, but it can also have serious effects on health. We have known for years that being depressed increases the risk of other serious illness, and, more recently, researchers have been able to detect a mechanism: being depressed reduces the functioning of our immune system.[5] Depression is best understood as a spectrum disorder—a continuum from feeling chronically "a little blue" to an incapacitating condition.

Depression can be evaluated by a number of scales. One of the most widely accepted is the Beck Depression Inventory.[6] But you can also monitor your own emotional "temperature" by paying attention to these important warning signs: increased use of alcohol or drugs, changes in "vegetative signs" (trouble getting to sleep, trouble staying asleep, waking up in the early morning and being unable to return to sleep, marked decrease or increase in appetite, or changes in energy level), rapid shifts in mood, persistent thoughts of injuring yourself or someone else, and interference with normal thinking and memory (increase in confusion, rumination—dwelling on the same thoughts over and over again, forgetfulness, and a slowing of thought processes). Even though emotional stress can produce brief instances of any of these symptoms, if you find that the symptoms persist more than two weeks, we recommend that you seek professional help. It can also be useful to have friends "check-in" with you regularly to help you monitor yourself.

We have found it helpful to remember that depression has a number of "tricks" and that these tricks can be countered. Depression's first trick is to see things in "all-or-nothing" terms: "I lost my job. That means I am a complete failure. That means I'll never get a decent job again." Notice that even though the first of the three sentences is undeniable, the next two do not follow logically—in fact, they are quite distorted. The loss of a job does not mean that you are a "complete failure," nor does it preclude future employment. To counter these distortions, remind yourself that rarely are things all black or all white. Look for the shades of gray.

Begin to enumerate counterexamples, such as, "It's true that I lost my job and that hurts. But there are many things that I do well, like playing the piano, being a trustworthy friend, cooking a mean spaghetti sauce, having a good tennis backhand, and so on." Start with skills that are not directly job-related, then work up to an enumeration of your job skills—"I type sixty words a minute, can use some spread-sheet and word-processing programs, have experience managing a small office, and so on." You may be surprised at the length of your list.

Depression's next trick is to constrict your time frame, that is, to collapse the past and foreclose the future, so that all you think about is the misery that you presently feel. It becomes difficult to plan and harder still to hope. To counter this, first remind yourself that this is a trick—that your past successes are still as real as they were before you felt depressed and that the future is still open to possibility.

Review your accomplishments. We have found it helpful for some people to look at old photo albums to remind themselves of the good times they have experienced and also of their effect on others. You may not have noticed your positive impact on others. Seeing their smiles may remind you. Remember that you have had sad times in the past but that they were followed by periods of joy as well.

Most important, begin to expand your future perspective. That is, "stretch" your thinking into the future. What would you like to be doing six months from now? A year from now? Imagine yourself happy in six months and looking back on the present. What advice would your happy self give to your sad and discouraged self now? What do you imagine you will think about this period a year from now?

Depression also tricks you into focusing on only the negative aspects of a situation. This may help you notice and anticipate dangers, but it can also badly skew your perceptions. You see everything that is wrong or ugly. You ignore everything that is right or beautiful. When you prune a rosebush, it is necessary to be aware of the thorns, but if you stop to count the thorns, you may miss out on the fragrance and beauty of the roses.

Depression's tricks are insidious and powerful. If you feel that depression has the upper hand, involve someone else to help you—a friend, a clergy person, or a caring professional.

The Power of Repetition

There is an old psychoanalytic saying that each loss recapitulates every loss. That is, whenever we suffer a loss it reminds us of every other loss we have suffered but not "digested." The emotional intensity that we feel from our current loss is amplified, and the pain of old losses is revisited.

This can be a serious problem when you have suffered extreme loss. There is scientific evidence of a "kindling" effect: suffering a traumatic experience sensitizes you and makes you *more* vulnerable to the effects of the next trauma.[7] When the loss has been unusually traumatic and you have felt intense fear, horror, or helplessness, you may experience symptoms of posttraumatic stress disorder (PTSD). Although many people think of PTSD only in the context of combat veterans, PTSD symptoms can often be found in survivors of natural disasters, auto accidents, crimes of violence, and those who were sexually abused as children.

Some of the symptoms of PTSD are similar to those of depression. But the most characteristic symptoms are distinctive and include "flashbacks" or other intrusive images of the traumatic situation, heightened physiological arousal (sweating, pupil dilation, rapid heart beat, etc.), increased startle response, and excessive vigilance.

When a person who is already suffering from PTSD is scapegoated, they may slink away in despair or explode in rage. In either case, the intensity of the reaction is likely to be exaggerated by the effect of past experiences. Fortunately, the last ten years have brought a number of promising new treatments to help resolve PTSD.[8] If you know that you have suffered past traumas that are contributing to your current situation, it is important to get professional help before moving to your next job.

Combating Depression by Self-Care and Self-Talk

One of the keys to helping yourself recover from scapegoating is to make your own health a priority. Many scapegoats make their focus getting another job as soon as possible. While this may be necessary economically, it is important to recognize that success in the future also depends on protecting your physical and emotional health.

Even relatively simple interventions, like moderate physical exercise, have been shown to help relieve depression.[9] Avoid the urge to spend your day in front of the TV. Instead, take walks, go to the gym, weed the garden—engage in some physical activity.

Researchers have noted that when we are depressed we tend to crave more carbohydrates.[10] Pay attention to your diet. Consider increasing the amount of water that you drink, decreasing caffeine (including caffeinated sodas), and adding vitamins, especially vitamins C and B complex (so-called "stress" vitamins). Remember that alcohol and most recreational drugs *depress* the central nervous system either directly or by a "rebound" effect.

Locate and commit to at least one pleasurable activity every day. Even if you don't feel like doing anything "fun," promise yourself to do it. You can involve family and friends to help by reminding and encouraging you. Read a novel, take a walk, enjoy the beauty of nature, call a friend for a cup of tea—find something that will please you. Turning your mood around is a little like using an old-fashioned pump: it needs to be primed.

Dealing with Rage

When we are threatened, one response is to take vigorous action in self-defense. When we enter the "fight" mode of our evolutionary "fight, flight, or freeze" response, several important things happen. A cascade of chemical messengers sends blood to the large muscles in our limbs, heart and respiration rates increase, pain threshold is raised, and inflammatory hormones flood into the bloodstream to prepare for wounds. Psychologically we move quickly from the experience of danger and fear to the experience of anger or rage. While anger has a mobilizing effect on our actions, it also usually disorganizes our thinking. In *Emotional Intelligence*, Daniel Goleman calls this process "emotional hijacking." The subcortical brain mechanisms that make emergency muscular activity and strength available also interfere with evaluating alternatives, strategizing, taking in the big picture, and so on—all the things you associate with higher cognitive function. The best (and most dangerous) martial artists are those who do not get angry, but instead methodically analyze and counter their opponents.

Don't make important decisions while you are in the grip of rage. Take a "timeout" and go for a walk, practice deep breathing, sit and meditate—agree with yourself that you will come back to your decision making when you are in your "right mind," that is, when you have your *entire* range of abilities to plan, analyze, and strategize. If you had to lift a heavy object, you would want to use *all* your strength—both of your arms, both of your legs, the muscles of your stomach and back, all working together. You would focus, check your posture, and "set" yourself before you began to lift. Do the same for making "heavy" decisions.

To cope with the urge to retaliate, remember the big picture. Think strategically. Remember to ask yourself, What is my goal? When you are being treated badly by an ill-intentioned person, ask yourself, Is this person *worth* my getting in trouble?

Dealing with Shame

Because work is a social situation, being disciplined or fired is also a social event. It directly affects your membership in the social group. So it is a situation ripe for the experience of shame, which is, as we saw in chapter 4, a basic social emotion. When we are shamed, we feel a desire to escape from the view of others and to hide. Hiding increases our isolation and delays healing.

To counter this impulse, recognize that you are not alone—this is one of the main purposes of this book. When you are feeling ashamed, you believe you are blameworthy and "bad." You may think that no one else has ever gone through this and that you are carrying a badge of singularity—you stand out from the group, exposed as not-good-enough. You want to hide. Hiding saves you from the acute embarrassment. You feel a little better when you hide, and this makes you more likely to continue to hide—at least for a while.

But hiding also reinforces the notion that you have done something wrong. That happens because you are always trying to make sense of your world. A kind of automatic process occurs, just below the surface of awareness. This process happens very quickly in the mind, and often in the form of telegraphic sentence fragments.[11] It goes something like this: "I'm hiding. There must be a good reason I'm hiding. It's so people won't see I was bad. I'm bad. I'd better keep hiding." When you become aware of this line of (erroneous) "reasoning," you can take steps to contest it. Check each of the "premises" and challenge them. Are they really logically connected or do they "slide" into one another? Ask what evidence there is to support or refute them. For example, even if you did *do* something "bad," it does not mean that you *are* "bad." Think about all the "good" things that you have also done. Counter your tendency to overgeneralize by asking yourself for specific instances of each. Notice how "good" and "bad" often represent social judgments, and become aware of *whose* standards you are accepting to make those judgments. Consider alternatives. For instance, you might be hiding not because you're "bad," but because someone else was out to hurt you.

Remember that the tendency to see things in "all-or-nothing" terms is a normal developmental stage (see chapter 4). But if your thinking gets stuck in that stage, it is easy to become a partner in the "dance" of scapegoating. That is, when a system seeks to cope with uncomfortable differences by projecting and attacking them, it may be easy for you to slip into the scapegoat role. The role is familiar—we can even say "familial"—because it is likely that you learned to do this very early. Because the family is the first representative of the group or collective, it is also the first arena for the social experience of shame.

The antidote for shame, and the associated desire to hide, is *exposure plus caring*. Telling others who care about you and finding out that they still care about you begins to undo the damage of shame and helps mobilize energy for moving back out into the social world of work. Since shame is a purely social emotion (i.e., it requires the presence of at least one other), it can only be cured in a social relation. Exposure plus caring helps to reintegrate the individual into the group.[12]

Remember Jack's fear (in chapter 1) of telling his wife and children? He was so ashamed that he even considered suicide rather than having to "expose" his "failure." Their acceptance did not miraculously make him better, but it set the foundation for his recovery. Involving a loving community (friends, church, or other groups of which you are a member) begins to expand the circle.

Planning for Recovery

"Make a new plan, Stan"—Paul Simon, 50 Ways to Leave Your Lover

Making a coherent plan involves analyzing what went wrong and beginning to formulate a new strategy (see chapter 9). It requires information. Review your "inventory" (see chapter 7) and your goals, priorities, and values (see chapter 8). Do you detect any patterns in the last three jobs you have held? This is a place where consultation with a professional can be especially valuable.

What are you looking for in your next workplace? Allow yourself to brainstorm. List the three most important qualities to you, regardless of how "realistic" they seem. For instance, "a sense of genuine caring about workers as people" might be on your list. Or "a chance to do my job without worrying about office politics." Whether it will be easy to find such a workplace is not the issue. The point of the exercise is to provide an awareness of the issues that are important to *you* so that you can conduct your job search with open eyes and so that you can learn more about yourself.

The Chinese character for "crisis" contains the characters for "danger" and "opportunity." Your job search may be a time of anxiety, but it gives you an opportunity to consciously explore and expand your personal skills. Let's look at this further, using Jack as an example.

Jack looked at himself in the mirror as he straightened his tie. He felt like a teenager getting ready to go out on a date. It had been a difficult month. First he'd had to prepare and update his résumé. Just looking at his old company's name on the page had sent waves of shame and fear through him. How would he explain to a prospective employer that he had been fired? He talked it over with his therapist. One of the things they discussed really stuck with him—that his tendency to accept blame, even when it wasn't appropriate, made him a very convenient target, and perhaps even encouraged others to heap more blame onto him. If he went into an interview with this attitude, he would be unlikely to get a job, or worse yet, he might find himself again in a situation where he would be identified, blamed, and banished.

He and his therapist had identified areas of competence where Jack truly felt confident in his abilities and other places where he knew he needed to develop his skills. Jack was beginning to take a more differentiated view of his own performance. While his confidence still felt shaky, Jack knew that he could honestly say that he and his former company were not a good "fit." Jack had sent out résumés to a number of companies and was surprised to have been offered several interviews. He was still terrified to face a prospective employer, but his therapist suggested that he approach an interview simply as "practice." This seemed to help. With a final check in the mirror, Jack picked up his résumé and walked to the door.

When he arrived at the new company, he was greeted pleasantly by the receptionist and asked to take a seat and wait. He took a couple of deep breaths to slow down his pounding heart and began to look around. He saw a busy office, with people moving quickly from cubicle to cubicle. It looked a lot like dozens of offices he had seen before. He noticed, though, that nobody was smiling. He also noticed that people tended not to look at each other as they passed in the corridors. One or two of them shot a glance in his direction and then quickly looked away. He wondered if he was just feeling overly sensitive and a bit "gun-shy."

This reverie was interrupted by the receptionist calling his name and ushering him into an inner office where the selection team was seated around a large table. He was introduced to the company vice president, the chief personnel officer, and the supervisor of the department in which he would be working. After a few pleasantries, the vice president asked Jack why he would like to work for their company. Jack was ready for this, and indicated his interest in the company's business and in applying his skill set to new tasks. More questions followed and the interview seemed to Jack to be going pretty well. When the department supervisor asked Jack why he had left his previous employer, Jack gave his rehearsed answer: "My previous company and I weren't a good fit." Feeling a rush of adrenaline, Jack asked the supervisor, "Could you tell me how this position came to be open?"

Out of the corner of his eye, Jack thought he saw the personnel officer stiffen but quickly resume his impassive demeanor. The department supervisor just grinned and said, "The previous employee wasn't a good fit in our department."

A few months ago, Jack would have jumped to meet the implied challenge. Now he just smiled back politely and realized that his job search might be a bit more extended and complex than he had expected.

There were a number of warning signs that this workplace might be trouble: people not smiling or looking at each other as they passed in the corridors, their curious but anxious looks at Jack, the apparent tension between the personnel officer and the job supervisor, and the snide response by the supervisor (echoing and subtly mocking Jack's answer). While no single sign guaranteed failure, together they were a powerful warning to Jack that he might be entering another treacherous situation.

Think about a job as a relationship. This doesn't mean that you will have to "marry" your workplace, but there are some important parallels between your work and personal life. First, you need to find a job that you can accept "as is." Just as it is a mistake to believe that you can remake your spouse, don't expect to change the job. Second, don't take a job (or a personal relationship) where *you* have to change more than you are willing, or one where the changes you want to make in yourself will take a long time—you probably won't have enough time, and may be branded a "failure." Try the following exercises.

Write Your "Personals Ad"

Imagine that you were reentering the dating world after the painful breakup of a long relationship. How would you present yourself? What would you write to describe yourself in a personals ad? There are more parallels than you might think.

What might interest or intrigue a potential new partner? ("World traveler; experienced manager"?) What do you do well? ("Avid hiker, loves opera, can write Linux"?) How do you think you will look to that new partner? ("Responsible and mature" or "over-the-hill"?) What are *you* looking for in a partner? What is your bottom line? ("nonsmoking vegetarian, blond, good benefits package"?)

Prepare a "Countertrance"

When we act on the basis of old patterns, or when we ignore readily available information, we are operating in a kind of a "trance." Behavior is automatic, unquestioned, and, by-and-large, not subject to critical awareness. While the best defense is awareness, it may also be useful to anticipate your tendency to slide back into archaic and automatic patterns and to develop mechanisms to counter such tendencies.[13]

Some people do this with "affirmations"—short sentences or phrases that counter the subvocal "automatic thoughts" that militate against success. For instance, you might approach a job interview thinking: "They'll see me as a failure. I have no chance." These thoughts may be very rapid and even barely noticeable—all you notice is the knot in your stomach and the flush in your face. It takes a conscious effort to oppose the negative self-talk by affirming: "I have many skills and many successes. Some company will be lucky to have me." Be realistic in your affirmations (i.e., don't claim to have invented the Internet if you didn't), but be *positive*. Daily practice will help to establish "balanced" thoughts as automatic.

Another way to think about this is to use the analogy of coaching. Most of us have had coaches of one sort or another in our lives. Some were lousy—they yelled, criticized, and demeaned us. Some were excellent—they encouraged, taught, believed in us, and exhorted us to do better than we imagined that we could.

Invite the excellent coach to accompany you in your mind. Visualize success. Take every interview as a chance to practice your skills. Imagine a baseball analogy and take the advice of a major leaguer— Barry Bonds, that is—"visualizing and clearing your mind" is the key.[14] Take a breath. Relax. When you are ready, step up to the plate. Keep your eye on the ball (your goals). After each at-bat (interview), critique your performance, and then let it go. Bonds says a fascinating thing: "Intensity slows you down. . . . It's a lot easier when you're relaxed." One way to reduce our intensity is to see the interview (or at-bat) as just one in a series of events. While each is important and deserving of our full attention, it is just one of many.

Think of the Interview as a "First Date"

A job interview, like a date, is an opportunity for each party to learn more about the other. Just like a date, both parties are usually on their best behavior. But this doesn't mean that important information is not being exchanged. In fact, some of the most important information has to do with the manner in which information is given. The *how* can be as important as the *what*. As we saw in Jack's interview, the nonverbal signals of tension between the personnel chief and the supervisor were as important as the stated reason that the position was open.

Interviewing is a two-way street. Your prospective employers are watching you as you watch them. But beware of "one-way" signs: deflections, subject changes, or glib rationalizations. These are signs of "taboo" areas; pursue them at your own risk. You can ask follow-up questions or return to the subject later, but you are signaling the other side that you have noticed something they may have been trying to conceal or gloss over. You may need the information to make a considered decision, but it may reduce your chances of being offered the position. When you challenge aspects of the culture before you are officially a member of that culture, you gain important information about the rules of the culture, but you make it harder to be accepted by them. Weigh the risks and benefits for yourself. Like a date, the process of "getting to know each other" can be mutually beneficial.

Jack approached his next interview with a little less trepidation—it was his third in the last two weeks, and he felt like he was beginning to get back into the swing of things. This was a smaller firm than he was used to, and he noticed with some interest that none of the parking spaces in the lot were reserved—a fact that had meant he had to park and walk a little farther than usual. Most of the employees seemed to know each other—they greeted each other by first name.

Looking around the office he noticed that the corner offices, at least the ones he could see, were not reserved for the executives, but in fact were conference rooms. He was ushered into one of these for his interview, where he shook hands with the personnel office, the chief executive, and two "team leaders." To his surprise, the receptionist who had brought him back to the interview room also stayed.

They asked Jack why he wanted to work for them, and Jack gave the speech that he had rehearsed and now given at several interviews. They listened politely and asked several questions about his experience and skills. Jack thought that some of their questions were things that they could have gotten from his résumé, but he answered them anyway. He felt like there were some other questions behind their questions, but he wasn't sure.

One of the team leaders talked about a project her group was working on and asked Jack if he had any ideas or reactions. Jack felt a little disarmed, but thought about it for a minute and responded by asking if they had considered a particular approach. The team leader smiled and said that they had just recently tried that, but hadn't been able to resolve the problem yet.

The second team leader and the receptionist both asked how Jack felt about a "team" approach to problem solving. Jack was used to a more hierarchical office organization, but said, honestly, that he had some interest in their approach. They asked if he could imagine that it would present any difficulties for him. Again Jack thought for a minute. He was feeling unusually at ease, but wasn't sure why. Maybe it was because the salary range for this position was at the low end of what he was looking for, and he had another interview lined up next week with a bigger company. Still, he sort of liked these people, so he screwed up his courage and answered: "I've always been a pretty private person, accustomed to doing my own work—and doing it well. I'm a little concerned that if the team doesn't get the job done, then I, as the new guy, will get blamed. But I'm intrigued, and willing to discuss this further." Jack was amazed at his own candor, but even more amazed at the smiles and nods that he saw in the faces around the table.

CHAPTER 11

Combating the Culture
of Scapegoating

Most of this book has been directed toward the individual victims of scapegoating. Since they have few advocates, this is appropriate. Along the way, however, we have offered information of benefit to astute managers—some of whom may also find themselves in the scapegoat role. In this last chapter, we address these two questions:

Why should management care?

If scapegoating is so embedded in society, how can we change the work-place?

The short answer to the first question is that companies, as well as individuals and society at large, are also "victims" of the process of scapegoating. To answer the second question, we address the larger, and, to our minds, more important issues of the roles of community and diversity in human life.

REVISITING THE COSTS OF SCAPEGOATING

In chapter 1 we established that scapegoating is not only psychologically costly, it can also have direct dollar costs to a company. Some of these costs come in the form of absenteeism, lost creativity and productivity, higher employee turnover, wrongful termination or harassment lawsuits, sabotage, and even workplace violence.

If the object of scapegoating has not already internalized and identified with the role, s/he is likely to experience such attempts at scapegoating as "harassment."[1] Data from a survey of a representative sample of U.S. employees studied during a one-year period (July 1992 to June 1993) revealed that verbal harassment of employees "can be even more destructive to employee productivity than a physical assault." This study, conducted by Northwestern Mutual Life Insurance Company, found that one out of four employees was the victim of harassment, threats, or physical attacks during the reporting period.[2]

Most of the costs are "externalized"—that is, they are not borne by the group that generates them, but rather by someone else—either the individual or society. A few of the costs, like higher premiums for workers' compensation insurance, are charged back to the individual workplace based on its history, but in the United States the companies involved do not usually directly pay the costs of scapegoating.

Many of the human costs are spread over the larger society in the form of health care premiums, social welfare expenses (cash payments for out-of-work families; the costs of intervention in domestic violence, child abuse, or neglect; vocational rehabilitation; and employment offices), and the cost of the legal system (both civil and criminal).

Individuals—particularly the scapegoated employees and their families—bear the primary emotional burden. Society may dismiss them as unfortunate "casualties" of a social process, but to do so is perilous on several grounds. First, seeing individuals as the problem blinds us to systemic problems and to possible solutions. We fail to see how the organization of the group itself produces the difficulty. Second, it blunts both our discernment and our compassion. Third, businesses lose important feedback about internal organizational problems. This makes it harder to attract and keep good workers.

We'll develop each of these ideas a bit more, but first let's take one last look at the fallout from the scapegoating phenomenon.

THE SCAPEGOAT AS INFORMANT

While scapegoating is a particularly destructive propensity in human social organization, it can also be a road sign that leads organizations to a better and more productive understanding of the structure of their business. Because scapegoating can function to define, distract, intimidate, or expiate, looking beyond scapegoating can alert an organization to an issue that is really in need of attention. For example, is the workgroup struggling to define itself? If so, this question can be addressed more positively and productively by stating *what the group is for* rather than *whom they are against*. Or if expiation (for real or imagined error) is the issue, there is a more productive fashion in which it can be addressed. (See the section on creating a "blame free" culture below.)

Noticing that your organization scapegoats is valuable information. It tells you that there is some other, crucial problem that is not being addressed directly. Until it is, the attention of the system will be misdirected, and the real problem will continue unchecked. The recognition of scapegoating should be a sign—like a flashing red light at an ungated railroad crossing—that some important information is available and that this information can be ignored only at great peril.

THE SCAPEGOAT AS HIDDEN TALENT

Social Darwinism—the "survival of the fittest"—is an increasingly difficult model to defend in our complex modern world. It is no longer so clear what characteristics are truly "adaptive" and valuable for survival.

For instance, brilliant minds can live in shattered or highly limited bodies. If survival depended on being able to outrun a predator, then the race (and survival) belongs to the swift. But if the survival of our group depends on understanding the world, then an individual who can think clearly and deeply may be of much more value to the species than a champion sprinter. What was adaptive for our distant ancestors may be irrelevant or even counterproductive in a modern industrialized society with a diverse, educated, multicultural population and workforce.

If we see scapegoats as "losers" in the dog-eat-dog world of business, we will have some trouble evolving beyond the mentality of the dog pack. Many creative individuals will leave businesses that continue to subscribe to this old dog-eat-dog model and will migrate to businesses that are more self-reflective and valuing of the gifts of a diverse workforce.

THE SCAPEGOAT AS JOURNEYMAN

Workers who have the most "transportable" (i.e., easily marketable) skills will leave jobs where they do not feel safe, and where the risk taking required of creative work may be punished. We have seen this in workplaces where innovation is stifled because experimentation must always be successful or the experimenter is blamed for "failure." If "failure" cannot be tolerated, there is a temptation to isolate and scape-goat those responsible for the failure.

In tight labor markets, like those in biotechnology, for instance, we see an increasing perception of need on the part of employers to offer a desirable and attractive work environment in order to attract and keep highly skilled workers who are in great demand. In an economy such as this, there is motivation to pay attention to the costs of scapegoating on a business's ability to attract workers who can choose among competing job offers. Unless high turnover is a managerial goal, attention to the emotional climate of the workplace is necessary. Applicants often know someone in the company offering them a job and are sensitive to the tenor of the workplace culture. As the highly successful entrepreneur Paul Hawkin states, "The best source of new employees is a satisfied worker."[3]

THE SCAPEGOATED MANAGER

Not all scapegoats are line workers. In fact, scapegoating can oc-cur at any level of an organization. Because it is a function of the cul-ture of the workplace, many managers scapegoat those who report to them because they themselves are scapegoated. Scapegoating becomes a kind of "pass-it-on" game. The process is embedded in the day-to-day modus operandi of the organization. Complaints by managers that executives are scapegoating them are not tolerated or are dismissed as "whining" or "avoiding responsibility." Responsibility is avoided for poor decision making at the highest levels of the organization, and vulnerable staff are driven out or otherwise "made to pay" for prob-lems that they had little or no part in creating. An extended example may help clarify this. We'll return to the job, and the manager who fired Jack.

Fred sat across from Alice, the director of Human Resources, and knew that despite her impassive demeanor, she was not pleased. So he began to explain. "Jack was a good worker in some ways, Alice, but we just couldn't keep him—he was undermining morale and just didn't fit in. Whiners have to go. I don't have time for them. But okay, okay. Human Resources is starting to talk about sending me for some 'man-agement training.' I know what that means. Some pencil pusher doesn't like my turnover statistics. So let's talk."

Alice asked about the content of Jack's complaints. Fred allowed that they were complaints he'd heard from others, and sometimes he even agreed with them. But there was nothing that he could do about the complaints. So he had tried telling Jack that if he wasn't happy here, he might be happier transferring. Jack had insisted that he wasn't the problem, the problem was with the department, and that rather than shutting him up, management ought to do something about the complaints, even if it meant sending them up through the ranks.

"Well, there is nothing I can do. This is how it is in business. We do the best with what we have. Period. If I start complaining to my boss about everything that I don't like here, I will be looking for a job, too. My boss is interested in the bottom line. He tells me, 'Don't just bring me your problems, bring me a solution at the same time or keep it to yourself.' That's how it is here—and everywhere else, I'm sure.

"One time Jack sat in the lunchroom going on and on about how the new vice presidents all get to park close to the building and how even twenty-year veterans here have to walk a long way through the parking lot to get to work. Everyone just sat there and stared at him. He called the vice presidents 'sacred cows.' Well, when you are in India you don't tell people to eat their sacred cows. He was always upset that things weren't fair."

Alice asked about Jack's relationships with his coworkers. Fred replied, "Well, Alice, he had a few friends, until he got so extreme and began to isolate himself. He did okay at first, but after awhile it was clear that he was kind of a hothead. In department meetings people would bring things up that they didn't like and ask him what he thought and he just couldn't let go of them once he got started. The others would mention them briefly, he wasn't the only one who had complaints, to be fair, but it seemed that he was always the one to take the ball and run with it. Sometimes I wondered if he was trying to be the official spokesperson for the group, but they would all look kind of uncomfortable and back away from him after he would take some strong stand on something. The rest of them had the sense to drop an issue when I would say there was nothing to be done about it, but in every meeting, like clockwork, the team would look at Jack like they knew he was going to say something more, and sure enough he would. After awhile, you could tell that the others didn't respect him. They would avoid him. If your coworkers don't like you, it is time to go—even if you do very good work—which he did, generally, though I must say that people began to notice mistakes he made more and more after awhile. Maybe he wasn't as competent as we thought either."

Alice asked, "Fred, what do you think about the fact that it was almost the same story with the last ones you let go? Good workers, generally, but who pointed out problems that others also pointed out—who *got into that role more than the others? I wonder if Jack was kind of a spokesperson for the group, but that they were afraid to back him up. After all, they had seen others terminated before him for doing the same thing. I know that you are pushed for productivity and that your managers don't care to hear about problems from you, but would things fall apart if you let them all complain sometimes, whether you can fix it or not?"*

Fred looked uncomfortable, glanced at his watch, and started to look through the papers on his desk. He hated whiners. They made him feel powerless. He felt obliged to fix the problems if he agreed that they existed, and wanted the employees to shut up if he didn't agree that the problem existed, as they were wasting his time and undermining morale. *"Alice, if it makes Human Resources happy, I will try it, but I don't look forward to my department meetings becoming whine sessions. I can't see how opening up cans of worms and pouring them out on the table can help. We have a good productive team when we weed out the folks who don't buy in to our mission. I just can't see this going anywhere productive. Maybe you can run a 'bitch session' for them when I am not there and see if it helps."*

Alice paused. *"Fred, I'm happy to meet with your people, but I think that one of the problems is this: listening to complaints without solutions feels like going downhill to you. Try listening without fixing everything. You might want to be there, and I will facilitate the meeting. Your employees are smart; they know you can't fix everything. We can also look at whom you are hiring. Do they know what they are getting into? The fifty- and sixty-hour weeks aren't for everyone. You need to make it very clear what the constraints are on the job here, that delivering products that still need a little 'tweaking' is standard, that productivity is central, and that the pay is commensurate.*

"But I think the problem is not hiring, Fred. I think that part of the problem is that we are all under a lot of pressure, and no one is allowed to complain. The generals are afraid of a mutiny. The unions are cold-calling our workers, asking them if being 'exempt' is really such a good deal. And things are not perfect here. We do need to improve. We need to develop ways for the people who get called the 'whiners' here to get their ideas thought through in a serious way. Sometimes the best process improvements come from these folks, who are often seen as the 'oddballs' because they do think differently. Let's see if we can sort out the difference between the people who are the genuine crackpots—who I would bet are rare—and those who are different and not afraid to say what is on their minds. Often they are pushed, behind your back,

by their coworkers, to speak up. But no one steps in to back them up when we tell them to pack up and go. Let's look at this more closely."

COMPETITIVE ADVANTAGE

In doing the research for this book, we found that the Europeans, particularly the British and the Scottish, have acknowledged "workplace bullying" and a process that they call "mobbing" that is close to what we have described as scapegoating. They have heightened public awareness of these problems and discussed ways to intervene. In many ways they appear ahead of the United States in their commitment to do something about this problem.

Although it is difficult to know why they are so far ahead, at least in terms of publicizing this problem, it is interesting to conjecture that it has to do with the internalization of what are externalized costs in the United States. In the European Economic Union, health care costs and many of the social welfare costs are built-in to the economics of running a business. If European businesses have to pay more of the *costs* of scapegoating, it is in their economic interest to prevent it. Companies that cannot continue to externalize human (or environmental) costs become more effective at using system "symptoms" such as workplace violence or workers' compensation claims as a tool for self-diagnosis and systemic improvement.

As the economy becomes more globalized, there is likely to be increasing tension between economies that internalize and those that externalize the costs of maintaining a healthy workforce. Agreements like the North American Free Trade Agreement (NAFTA) *externalize* costs—such as the effects of toxic waste pollution—by shifting production to countries with fewer environmental and labor protections. Other models advocate that a company that produces a societal cost (like the health effects of smoking cigarettes) be responsible for paying for it.[4] It is difficult to predict how the balance will be struck between these models.

We can hope that greater awareness of the real costs will increase public demands for accountability. If this does come to pass, companies that have already taken steps to reduce the cost of scapegoating will be at a competitive advantage.

There is another, equally important competitive consideration. As the market becomes more global, the need to be able to understand and respond to the needs of different clients increases. A company that does not tolerate "difference" within its own ranks will have great difficulty understanding or tolerating the differences it will encounter in a global market. We have more to say about this later in this chapter.

CORPORATE "CITIZENSHIP"

Any first-year law student can tell you that a corporation is a fictional *entity*: a group that "incorporates" is forming a "body" ("corpus" in Latin) that is entitled to many of the same legal protections as an individual citizen. But the notion that corporations, like individuals, have some moral obligation to the community in which they live is less accepted.

As long as there was a "frontier," it was easy to maintain the notion of limitless potential. However, in an increasingly crowded global "village" it is difficult to maintain the fiction that corporations can afford to ignore the communities in which they are situated and simply "move on" like restless individuals if they are dissatisfied. Phil Wander, a professor of linguistics at San Jose State University, has noted that "unlimited growth is the ideology of cancer."[5] Instead, sustainability will have to become the watchword of development in the twenty-first century. This means conserving human as well as material resources. Both are, of course, replaceable—but only at rates that allow for the development of replacements. Strategies that preserve and develop human resources serve a societal as well as a corporate good. Scapegoating is destructive of both.

Let's turn now to a discussion of our second question.

If scapegoating is so embedded in human social nature, how can we possibly avoid it in the workplace?

We have argued that the tendency to scapegoat is rooted in three major areas: the human unconscious, the nature of human social groups, and the typical organization of profit-seeking businesses. The unconscious mind deals with unacceptable thoughts by projecting them "out" onto another person or object. The human group defines itself by creating boundaries between the "in-group" and the "out-group," by simplifying information via stereotyping and by ignoring information that does not fit the pattern of current group belief about its own "norms."

Businesses are groups that are driven by the search for financial profit. They have developed ways to be more competitive in the marketplace. These ways often are "convergent" —that is, they are refinements of what they are already doing and tend to narrow the focus, creating a bias against divergent ideas (unless they can be demonstrated to be profitable).

To avoid scapegoating it is necessary to expose projections, to create more permeable social boundaries, to learn to tolerate and absorb complexity an ambiguity, and to think divergently as well as convergently. Change is best instituted when it occurs at several levels simultaneously: the personal, the organizational, and the cultural. But often one level will predominate, and in the case of workplace behavior, change may need to be initiated at the top.

Human beings have many tendencies that are modified by the rules of social interaction. Social behavior is greatly influenced by the surrounding culture. One key to altering behavior is to alter the culture. But cultures are highly resistant to change.

Consider the cultural practices that supported racial segregation in Mississippi in the 1940s. First, there were formal legal barriers. These included a variety of "Jim Crow" laws that officially required separation of blacks and whites. Some of the laws were statewide; others were city ordinances. They included regulations such as separate entrances for different "races" into public buildings, separate rest rooms, separate sections in movie theaters, and even separate public drinking fountains. These regulations were buttressed by a poll tax that effectively excluded blacks from voting for the officials who made and enforced the laws.

Second, there were cultural practices that determined the proper social behavior expected of "colored" and "white" folks. These practices also included a community definition for what constituted disrespectful or insulting behavior. Such standards were enforced by a variety of extralegal social sanctions that culminated at the extreme end with beatings or even lynchings for breaches of unwritten but tacitly understood rules.

Third, there were widespread personal beliefs about the differences between the "races." Most of us are familiar with these: blacks have a natural sense of rhythm, are lazy, are hypersexualized, and so on, and that whites are more intelligent, diligent, and hardworking. Note that the lack of scientific evidence for these beliefs does little to discourage them. Instead they become self-fulfilling prophecies: if you expect someone is sexier, s/he is (since most researchers agree that the most highly developed human sex organ is the brain), and if you expect someone to say something intelligent, you may discount it as an aberration when s/he doesn't.

This triumvirate of laws, cultural practices, and personal beliefs created a system that was highly resistant to change. The law provided cover for the cultural practices and personal beliefs. The cultural practices and personal beliefs made it more likely that legislators would be elected who would codify the cultural practices and beliefs into law. This sort of vicious cycle can be broken at any level, but usually it occurs from the top down—that is, with a change in the law. In fact, this is what happened in Mississippi, when conflicts between federal and state laws were resolved in favor of the more egalitarian federal statutes.

Similarly, change in the culture of an organization often begins from the top. This can come in the form of new office policies, regulations, or procedures. Examples of these include policy statements regarding equal employment opportunity, nondiscrimination, and zero tolerance of sexual harassment.

Simply stating these policies is not sufficient to create a changed workplace. The changes are made "real" by the history of practices. These include a perceived commitment by the employer to the new policy. This commitment can be demonstrated by periodic reminders, memos, training, and so on, but is most effective when it is backed up with actual practice. Examples would be when a harassing manager is forced to attend "sensitivity training" in order to keep his job or when an abusive supervisor is disciplined or terminated because of repeated violation of stated policy.

To combat scapegoating in the workplace effectively, management needs to be clear that scapegoating is not a desirable practice and that they wish to oppose it. We hope that the bulk of this book has established the emotional, social, economic, and systemic undesirability of scapegoating. What is needed is recognition that alternatives are available and desirable and that management can hasten the actualization of a different way.

The cultural practices of the office need to be addressed as well. Are members of the workplace supporting each other in certain beliefs and practices in "extralegal" ways? For example, is there unofficial favoritism or a double standard? Is there support within the office for isolating, blaming, and excluding workers? Management can help raise awareness of this by directly addressing it in group meetings, and supervisors can comment on it immediately if they observe it happening. But perhaps the most effective way the culture can be changed is through modeling different behavior.

Much of social learning occurs vicariously—by observation of others, especially others whom we value or consider authorities. Two developmental social psychologists, Albert Bandura and Richard Walters, did a series of clever experiments that showed that aggressive behavior in children could be learned, reinforced, or elicited by watching adults behave aggressively.[6] Similarly, self-control, even in the face of frustration, could be learned by watching grown-ups behaving appropriately. The higher the status of the adult model, and the greater the association between the model and the ability to dispense rewards, the greater the likelihood that the child would imitate the adult's behavior.

The analogy to managerial behavior is obvious. Managers and supervisors have both prestige and access to dispensing rewards and punishments (in the form of promotions or demotions). So the behavior of the manager is likely to be closely observed. Does he or she "walk the walk"? It may be official policy to avoid scapegoating, but does he or she really avoid blaming, search for systemic solutions, and stay away from isolating, projecting, and excluding individual workers?

In the language of organizational development, this kind of modeling is part of what is called "leadership." The *performance* of the "performance leader" is crucial to the outcome of attempts to change the organization.[7] The leader must not only endorse but also embody the desired change.

Changing personal beliefs is the most difficult. Strongly held beliefs and prejudices may be outside the realm of workplace control. However, workplace behavior can be modified. Behavior regarding scapegoating may be changed by appealing to self-interest: no one wants him/herself to be scapegoated, and it can be made clear that scapegoating is like a prairie fire—once it gets established, it is very difficult to stop, and it can in turn destroy the property of the "innocent" as well as the "guilty." Again, the managers need to model nonblaming problem-solving behavior. Modeling by managers is a relatively quick way to change organizational culture. Espousing one thing and doing another is a quick and certain way to create confusion, distrust, and low morale.

COMPASSION

Compassion is the ability to put yourself emotionally in the position of the other. It is *not* pity. It is an emotional understanding of the predicament of the other—an empathic understanding that also accepts that suffering is a part of everyone's life. It does not mean giving up your own point of view, but rather being able to move back and forth, accurately, between another's point of view and your own.

This recognition of the universality of suffering can be very unsettling. It is often easier to imagine that the other's suffering is due to some error—technical or moral—on his/her part. Believing this, you can distance yourself from the other's pain. If instead you also feel that pain, blame tends to evaporate. One of the antidotes to blaming—and particularly to scapegoating—is compassion. Paul Hawkin shows us the wisdom of compassion toward our fellow workers in his admonition to managers: "Precisely because you and I are ordinary people with flaws as well as virtues, we must assiduously maintain respect for all associates."[8]

VALUING DIFFERENCE

Although not everything that is different is innovative, everything that is innovative is, by definition, different. Appreciating difference is also a way to maximize the problem-solving potential of a system. Creativity and innovation depend on the ability to think divergently as well as convergently, that is, to reexamine a problem from a fresh and perhaps unusual perspective and to coordinate multiple perspectives. Lani Guinier nicely summarizes this in her study of gender bias in America's system of legal education:

Problem solving, especially the solving of complex problems, may require individuals who not only value but need the input of diverse perspectives and skills, including the ability to listen not just speak, the ability to synthesize not just categorize, and a willingness to think hard about nuance and context even when that slows down the process of decision making. Indeed, among highly competent lawyers, successful performance often depends on a team of individuals, no single one of whom possesses all of the necessary expertise but all of whom, working together, are able to accomplish their task in a reliable way.

The most important lesson we learned, therefore, is that we must listen to the voices of those whose experience is both marginal and central to our understanding.[9]

Being "inclusive" is not only morally right, but also "practical"—it allows the coordination of multiple perspectives on a problem. How does a manager keep the conversation from becoming a confusing babble? By creating the expectation that all voices will be heard and by cultivating the view that all of the parties have *a common interest*, namely, solving the problem that affects all of them.

Learning to tolerate difference—in you as well as in another—is a developmental task. That is, it is part of becoming a complete and mature human being.

NOTICING THE SELF

Jungian psychologists write about the individual's *shadow*, the unacknowledged abilities, attributes, and personality traits that generally remain unconscious, but occasionally emerge into conscious life with a quality of the "not me." Jung summarized the dynamic and developmental nature of this by saying, "That shows there is always a part of our personality which is still unconscious, which is still becoming; we are unfinished; we are growing and changing."[10] Integrating this shadow can be painful. Remember our discussion of projection. Often shadow material is projected on to another and attacked. Taking back these projections means acknowledging things about yourself that you might not like. But the benefit of doing so is at least twofold.

First, it allows you to see social reality more clearly and accurately, which makes it more likely that you can be interpersonally effective. Second, it expands your repertoire of experience and behavior. You inhabit your own life more fully; you actively acknowledge aspects of your being.

As the acerbic psychologist Jay Haley suggests, it seems to be a law of social reality that in order to accept credit for something, you have to acknowledge your activity in desiring it.[11] This trade-off is beautifully summarized by the Jungian analyst James Hollis, who wrote: "Projections embody what is unclaimed or unknown within ourselves. Life has a way of dissolving projections and one must, amid the disappointment and desolation, begin to take on the responsibility for one's own satisfactions."[12]

We believe that systems, including businesses, also have a shadow side and that recognizing it is the first step to bringing the hidden potentials to consciousness, where their appropriate use can be decided. On a personal level, this can occur when a manager comes to an awareness and acceptance of his/her own flaws and virtues (see the Paul Hawkin quotation in the previous section). This makes it less likely that that manager will look for someone else to blame if things go wrong at work.

Another analogy may illustrate: A parent who accepts his/her strengths and weaknesses as a person and as a parent has less need to make a child the scapegoat for things that go wrong in the family. The child will be asked to carry his/her share of the responsibility (with an age-adjusted expectation) at the same time that the parents carry his/her own share of responsibility for things going well or badly.

A business that can be honest about its shortcomings ("We are growing so fast that our back office functions are disorganized; none of our managers has any real experience as a manager.") will not need to blame employees for problems in maintaining a fiction about its "self-image" as an organization. It will also be in a better position to deal realistically with its less developed aspects ("We probably need to devote some resources to management training to help our back office get up to speed."), as well as utilizing its existing strengths ("All our managers have been on the frontlines of development and production.").

NOTICING THE OTHER

There is a common tendency to mistake what is familiar with what is "normal" or "right." Because we have always done something a certain way does not mean that this is the only or the best way to do it. This process of accepting what is usual for what is normative contributes to social "stability"—but at the cost of devaluing what is different. Difference may or may not have immediate value to a system, but it provides alternative viewpoints.

If, as the French psychologist Jean Piaget suggests, intelligence is the ability to simultaneously coordinate multiple perspectives, then systems that can tolerate and utilize internal differences are more intelligent. As such, they are able to balance the structure of the system with the structure of the environment. In a complex world, flexible intelligence is necessary to respond to changes in a timely manner.

GRATITUDE

One of the emotional antidotes to resentment is gratitude. When we experience appreciation for our life situation—even for being alive at all—we often feel a sense of completion and tranquility that reduces dissatisfaction. This is captured in common sayings like, "Count your blessings" or, "Every cloud has a silver lining." This gratitude cannot be manufactured, and it is difficult to produce on demand. Sometimes it has the quality of what is called *Grace* in Christianity, *Baraka* in Islam, and *Samadhi* in Hinduism. It is a divine gift to the believer.

It *is* possible, however, to cultivate an attitude of appreciation and acceptance of yourself and of others. This involves noticing what is "right" as well as what is "wrong" in any situation. It also means reminding yourself of your own ability to choose. And it means seeing things in a differentiated, not an "all-or-nothing" fashion.

> *Roxanne was a middle manager in a department that was constantly under fire from upper management. Not only Roxanne, but also numerous line employees were "called on the carpet" by upper management and blamed for problems in the company's productivity. As a result morale fell, and so did production.*
>
> *Roxanne saw this and yet promoted an attitude of "curiosity"[13] to understand the department's problems and to prescribe another way to handle them. This meant informing upper management that the resources were inadequate to do the job, and holding open discussions with her employees on the reality of the "working lean and mean" culture. This also included the recognition that it was an exploitive work environment that invited codependence in order to be sustainable. She invited employees to take responsibility for working there—the pay and benefits were good—and to leave if the price tag was too high over time. Many with families did leave, and she did not count this against them when asked to provide letters of recommendation. The workforce composition changed—her department became mostly young, single workers who were ambitious and willing to work long hours. However, many of them were lured away by other firms dangling even sweeter pay and benefit packages. Consequently, her department had both high productivity and high turnover.*

Recognizing that you have a choice, even if it is a choice between unpopular options, is a way of recognizing your own role in actively shaping the course of your life. When you are actively engaged in your life, there is less room for the passive "victim." Knowing that you have chosen can be very frightening. But it is also an opportunity to celebrate your ability to choose. Gratitude does not erase awareness of inequity or injustice. But it does help to balance perception and avoid the all-or-nothing thinking that is so prevalent in depression and in scapegoating itself.

CULTIVATING TRUE CORPORATE DIVERSITY

We support the position taken by Peter Senge and Margaret Wheatley that asks individuals to take responsibility for organizational culture.[14] This may mean using a union or management forum or a consultant. It will probably mean not acting alone to try to change an organization's mores, unless you are at a very high level in the organization. We advocate a position of proactive structuring of the workplace, rather than a "victim" stance toward organizational culture. Unions have, over the last several decades, pushed businesses to accept disabled workers, women, minorities, and older workers into the workplace community over loud protests and deep resistance. The fears that the newly integrated employees would be inferior to the white males who dominated the workplace did not materialize. Gradually workplaces have accommodated working parents, employees from other cultures, and those who needed part-time work or to telecommute. The business world is starting to reflect the larger culture and its diversity.

THE VALUE OF CREATIVE DISSENT

Just as the American Constitution protects dissent in the interests of a more perfect process of self-rule, businesses, to be successful in a rapidly changing world, must do the same. Freedom of speech is so important because we recognize the temptation toward tyranny of those who support whatever the current dominant paradigm is at the time.

Paradigm shifts are inevitable, but need not be violent or sudden revolutions. Extreme polarizations need not extract their terrible price on those on either side of the dialectic if a commitment to hearing from all stakeholders and valuing the truth in multiple points of view can be maintained. Scapegoating is a classic and ancient way to try to repress any attempt to challenge or modify the current dominant paradigm, be it business orthodoxy or religious or political orthodoxy.

The nineteenth-century British political philosopher John Stuart Mill was influenced by the ideas of the American Revolution. He made a telling argument for diversity in his famous essay, "On Liberty."[15] In it he argues that since no one can claim to know with absolute certainty what "truth" is, that no government can rightly limit discussion or argument. If what we know as "truth" is only the argument that currently demonstrates the clearest logic or the most evidence, then we must always be open to the possibility of a better argument or more compelling evidence. The more that we limit the expression of opinion, the greater our chance of error.

We can bring Mill's argument into the workplace: the more we suppress dissenting views, the greater our chances of proceeding down a mistaken path. W. Edwards Deming was fond of pointing out that the reason many excellent automotive carburetor companies went out of business was because "they saw themselves as carburetor makers, not as providers of mixing fuel and air."[16] That is, they were thinking convergently—how to improve the performance of their product, how to streamline production, how to ensure quality control, and so on, rather than divergently—what was the purpose of the device they were making and could a radical redesign create a new and superior product, namely, the fuel injector.

LEARNING TO TOLERATE DIFFERENCE (ONE SIZE DOES NOT FIT ALL)

Angeles Arrien defines diversity in a very useful way. She reminds us that "many Native American cultures hold a belief that each individual is . . . 'original medicine,' nowhere else duplicated on the planet."[17] This fits with the information from modern genetics that each individual (with the exception of monozygotic or identical twins) is a *unique* genotype—there is no one with exactly the same genetic information. Each person's contribution toward the whole is important in the ecosystem of the community. Redefining the workplace to reflect the broader community and to meet its needs, rather than to simply have an exploitative relationship with it, is one of the functions of "deep diversity." Race, class, gender, and culture are but a few manifestations of the different aspects of diversity. Different perceptual and valuing styles are well documented in the literature, and many employers try deliberately to build a balance of these styles and skills in a given work team using personality tests.

One of the commonly used assessment measures is the Meyers-Briggs Type Indicator.[18] This instrument is based on the Jungian theory of personality types. It classifies individuals according to four aspects of their dominant mode of knowing and relating to the world—introverted or extraverted, thinking or feeling, sensing or intuiting, and judging or perceiving. There are sixteen possible combinations or "types," and each has a somewhat different set of interests, values, needs, and abilities. Each brings particular strengths to a team, as well as particular "blind spots." For example, an extraverted-feeling type might be more successful in tasks that require meeting new people, like sales or marketing, while an introverted-thinking type might do better in research and development. However, both types might work effectively together as long as they could realize that their different styles were not better or worse, just *different*.[19]

CREATING A "NO-BLAME" CULTURE

Removing the notion of blame does *not* remove the concept of responsibility. Rather it indicates a willingness to examine and learn from experience and even from blunders. The morbidity and mortality conferences that are held regularly in hospitals are an example. Cases are presented and explored with the purpose of determining how future bad outcomes might be prevented or ameliorated. No formal record of the proceedings is kept. The attitude of such meetings is serious and sometimes competitive, as no one likes to acknowledge that they might have made an error or overlooked an alternative, especially if it led to a patient's death. However, these meetings often result in the advancement of the knowledge of everyone present *and* in the immediate improvement of patient care. If participants were humiliated or punished, it is unlikely that anyone would attend voluntarily or participate openly.

A similar model has been described for evaluating aircraft disasters.[20] Whether the crash occurred due to pilot error, mechanical failure, unforeseen weather conditions, and so on, the complexity of events leading to the disaster is unlikely to be truly understood unless all participants, and outside experts, can speak freely, without concern of recrimination.

In ordinary business, decisions and mistakes are not likely to be matters of life or death. We use these dramatic examples to illustrate that even extreme errors can produce changes that benefit society or a business. But this can only happen in an atmosphere that values all information, even information that is embarrassing or incriminating. People are more likely to be honest when they do not fear reprisal. Max DePree, CEO of the furniture design and manufacturing company Herman Miller, Inc., writes, "Without forgiveness, there can be no real freedom to act within a group."[21]

Businesses can create an atmosphere that encourages their members to honestly evaluate a situation. Management needs to make it clear that the goal is understanding and improving the product or service—*not* assigning blame for failure. Only then is it likely that all the relevant information will come to light. Scapegoating only derails this process.

GLOBAL MARKETING

If you want to sell to the world, you had better understand your market. The infamous gaffe by General Motors, marketing the Chevy Nova in South America ("No-va" means "doesn't go" in Spanish), remains a classic humorous example of cultural misunderstanding. Many such examples are more serious.

It was once fashionable to denigrate other cultures, to see them as "less than" our own. Goods imported from Japan were once assumed to be shoddily made. Now Japanese autos are seen as setting industry standards for quality and reliability.

Good ideas do not know national boundaries. The views of an American industrial psychologist, W. Edwards Deming, were virtually ignored by U.S. industry.[22] But his ideas on quality, worker participation in decision making, and inventory control were highly influential in Japan and have contributed to its industrial renaissance.

A number of writers have suggested that the ethnic and cultural diversity of the United States, far from being a liability in a global market, is actually a powerful and largely ignored asset.[23] A diverse workforce is capable of flexibility and innovation and has the ability to identify and connect with different points of view. This positions it advantageously in a market that is fast changing and that requires communication with many different types of people. Instead of attacking difference as potentially "foreign," we can use it to increase productivity and connectedness.

SOME FINAL THOUGHTS ON WORKPLACE SCAPEGOATING

It is tempting to end this book with what is called an Executive Summary—a *very* brief overview of the main points, with emphasis on the "take home" or "action points"—that encapsulates the suggestions for change. Cramming this chapter into such a paragraph might read like this: Scapegoating is deeply rooted in the social and emotional organization of human beings. Scapegoating is expensive to business in many ways and is a luxury that modern businesses cannot afford. Efforts to counter scapegoating need to focus on the factors that encourage its expression. These include the need to define the group, to organize and motivate the workers, and to cope with mistakes and problems. Both workers and managers participate in being victims, victimizers, or witnesses to the process. Managers must become convinced of the disutility of scapegoating and must model different ways of solving systemic problems. Targets of scapegoating need to learn to recognize it quickly and to actively oppose the identification, isolation, projection, and exclusion that comprise the process. To avoid scapegoating, it is necessary to expose projections, to create more permeable social boundaries, to learn to tolerate and appreciate complexity and ambiguity, and to think divergently as well as convergently. All parties can benefit by valuing diversity and complexity in the workplace, in society, and in themselves.

It is the responsibility of everyone to recognize and oppose scapegoating. Recognition brings scapegoating out of the shadowy areas of our consciousness, where it smolders and grows, into the light of awareness, where its lessons about the problems of systems and individuals can be learned and where its destructive aspects can be confronted and contained.

For the system, this makes it more likely that the real reasons for difficulty can be identified, examined, and modified. This increases organizational efficiency, reduces unnecessary costs, and makes the workplace a more desirable environment for the employees.

For society, recognizing and eschewing scapegoating means taking a more differentiated view of the world and accepting responsibility for its own projections on the "other," be they the most recent immigrants to the country or the most recent international competitor or adversary. Whenever the term "enemy" is used, look again; examine what element of the society is being projected upon and subjected to attack. Examine the functions that the scapegoating is serving: cohesion, expiation, intimidation, or distraction.

For individuals, the act of opposition transforms them from victims in an ancient morality play into active, aware participants in their own drama. Even when the outcome is banishment, the conscious person can mourn the loss, but take some solace at the increase in his/her appreciation for the complexity of human social interactions, and for more fully inhabiting a precious, and time-limited life. These are accomplishments that are transportable—they can be used to make not only future employment, but also daily life, more rich, differentiated, and satisfactory.

Notes

CHAPTER 1

1. According to a study by Northwestern National Life Insurance Company, "Employee Burnout: America's Newest Epidemic," Minneapolis, MN: Author, 1991.

2. Princeton Survey Research Associates, "Labor Day Survey: State of Workers," Princeton, NJ: Author, 1997.

3. R.Z. Goetzl, D.R. Anderson, R.W. Whitmer, R.J. Ozminkowski, R. Dunn, and J. Wasserman, "The Relationship between Modifiable Health Risks and Health Care Expenditures: An Analysis of the Multi-employer HERO Health Risk and Cost Database," *Journal of Occupational and Environmental Medicine* 40, no. 10 (1998).

4. Joel H. Neuman, "Injustice, Stress, and Bullying Can Be Expensive!" Available at www.bullybusters.org/home/twd/bb/res/neuman4.html.

5. NIOSH publication no. 99-101, "Stress at Work," 1999. Also available at www.cdc.gov/niosh/stresswk.

6. Bureau of Labor Statistics, "National Census of Fatal Occupational Injuries, 1997," 1998.

7. While the motives of the two students who went on a murderous and tragic shooting rampage at Columbine High School in Colorado in 1999 are complex and may never be known, we do know that they had been isolated, marginalized, and ridiculed. That they participated in cultivating their "outsider" status does not lessen the tragedy for themselves or for their victims.

The phenomenology of rage has been studied at Duquesne University and, interestingly, one of its main components is a sense of "disembodiment." That is, rage is in part a way of attempting to force others to recognize one's physical being. Diminishing, ignoring, or dismissing another's physical presence is highly insulting and often provokes an outraged response.

CHAPTER 2

1. The King James translation of the Holy Bible.

2. See H.G. Liddel and R. Scott, *Greek Lexicon*, 7th ed., Clarendon Press, 1997, p. 855, which defines *pharmakos* as "one who is sacrificed as an atonement *for others*, a scapegoat." See also T. Gaster, *Myth, Legend and Custom in the Old Testament*, Harper & Row, 1969.

3. The conquering Romans noted human sacrifices in Europe. One form of ritual sacrifice involved enclosing victims in large wickerwork structures and burning them alive. This gave way first to substituting animal for human victims and finally to the more symbolic practice of stuffing the wickerworks with straw (and gave rise to our expression, "a straw man"). This practice was seen in midsummer and harvest rituals in Scotland, France, and Germany. It was gradually suppressed, sometimes by legal decree (as late as the eighteenth century), though symbolic vestiges can still be found in current celebrations. See James Frazer, *The Golden Bough*, London: Wordsworth, 1933 (originally published in 1922).

4. Robin Bulman, "Analysis: Blaming Ex-leaders Is Popular in S. Korea," *Reuter News Service*, July 11, 1998.

5. James Frazer wrote *The Golden Bough* in twelve volumes. It is the classic study of magic and sacrifice in human myth and history. While Frazer relied on anthropological evidence that has since been heavily criticized, several aspects of his argument are particularly relevant for our discussion. First is the role of imitation in ritual. The ritual participant mimics the appearance or attributes of the desired totem or god in order for the power of the totem to be *transferred* to the participant. The whole is induced by the production of a part. This is a variant of the process of part/whole confusion that exists in the normal development of thought (see our chapter 4). Second is the notion of magical contagion. That is, physical proximity can produce a *transfer* of attributes, positive or negative. It is tempting to see this as an empirical finding based on the observation of the spread of illness in a community. When the pathogens are invisible and the vector unknown, we are left with the observation that those closest to the ill are also the most likely to fall ill.

Both part/whole thinking and contagion are important aspects of scapegoating. Scapegoats are often identified by one or more "bad" characteristic that comes to stand for the totality of their being. This process of caricature is often seen in political cartoons. Magical contagion is directly linked to the scapegoating process, as the community tries to cope with its "illness" by isolating and excluding the individual who has been identified as "bad." Associating with this identified "problem" risks being labeled "bad."

6. Ibid.

CHAPTER 3

1. This can be seen most poignantly in the studies done by the British psychoanalyst John Bowlby, in which children were separated from their parents. See *Attachment and Loss*, Vol. 3, *Loss: Sadness and Depression*, Basic Books, 1980. After prolonged separations, some of the children became profoundly depressed and withdrawn, and even the return of their parents could not rouse them from their lethargy.

2. Our word *shibboleth*, a word used as a test, comes from the biblical story (Judges 12:6) of the conquering Gileadites who distinguished escaping Ephraimites from other refugees by asking them to pronounce the word. The unfortunate Ephraimites couldn't make the initial "sh" sound and were killed.

3. Gregory Bateson, *Steps to an Ecology of Mind*, Ballantine, 1972.

4. Solomon Asch did the pioneering studies of this in the 1950s. See his "Studies of Independence and Conformity," *Psychological Monographs* 70, no. 9 (whole no. 416) (1956).

5. S. Milgram, *Obedience to Authority*, Harper & Row, 1974. Milgram's work shocked many readers and sparked a debate among psychologists about the ethics of experimentation.

6. In these experiments, a mock prison was set up, and some subjects (all "normal" young men who volunteered and were to be paid $15/day for their participation) were randomly assigned the role of "guards" and others "prisoners." The experiment had to be curtailed about halfway through the scheduled two weeks as the "guards" began inventing ways to humiliate and degrade the "prisoners," and some of the prisoners began to show signs of severe emotional and physical distress. Roles exerted such a powerful influence on behavior that participants "forgot" that all that they had to do to gain their release was to say that they wanted to leave the experiment.

The research was done in 1971 and originally reported in C. Haney, W.C. Banks, and P.G. Zimbardo, "Interpersonal Dynamics in a Simulated

Prison," *International Journal of Criminology and Penology* 1 (1973): 69–97. The importance of the experiment is revisited in C. Haney and P.G. Zimbardo, "The Past and Future of U.S. Prison Policy: Twenty-five Years after the Stanford Prison Experiment," *American Psychologist* 53 (1998): 709–27. A slide and video presentation on the experiment is also available at www.zimbardo.com/prison/htm.

7. Robert Sapolsky discusses this in *Why Zebras Don't Get Ulcers*, W.H. Freeman, 1998. The effects of overcrowding on rat populations are vividly described by J.B. Calhoun in "A Behavioral Sink" in *Roots of Behavior*, ed. E.L. Bliss, Harper & Row, 1962.

8. Human responses to crowding are extremely complex and seem to involve "calculations" of the utility of aggressive responses. People also vary in the degree of distress that physical crowding produces. A nice review of this complexity is available in I. Altman, *The Environment and Social Behavior*, Brooks/Cole, 1975.

9. Renee Girard, *The Scapegoat*, Johns Hopkins University Press, 1986.

10. W. Bion, *Experiences in Groups*, Basic Books, 1961.

11. For an excellent review of this, see L. Malcus, "In the Beginning: Biblical and Psychodynamic Bases of Scapegoating." Paper presented at the 55th Annual Conference of the American Group Psychotherapy Association, Chicago, IL, 1998.

12. Sigmund Freud, *Moses and Monotheism*, Standard Edition 23, New York, 1939.

13. D. Bakan, *Disease, Pain and Sacrifice*, Beacon Press, 1968.

14. J. Lacan, *The Four Fundamental Concepts of Psychoanalysis*, W. W. Norton, 1973.

15. J. Jaynes, *The Origins of Consciousness and the Breakdown of the Bicameral Mind*, Houghton-Mifflin, 1976.

16. Ibid.

17. Consider that the branding of criminals continued into the nineteenth century in the United States, and still continues in some parts of the world today. The brand serves not only as a warning to others to beware of the criminal, but also as an indelible mark of shame to separate the offender from the rest of society.

18. M. Sherif, O. Harvey, B. White, and W. Hood, *Intergroup Conflict and Cooperation: The Robbers Cave Experiment*, Institute of Group Relations, University of Oklahoma, 1961. In this fascinating study, psychologists set up several summer camps for youngsters around a lake and explored how rivalries between the groups accelerated the formation of group cohesion.

CHAPTER 4

1. H.S. Sullivan, *The Interpersonal Theory of Psychiatry*, W.W. Norton, 1953. See also more modern work on the importance of nonverbal communication between parents and infants, M.H. Klaus and J.H. Kennell, *Parent-Infant Bonding*, Mosby, 1982.

2. A. Miller, *The Drama of the Gifted Child*, Basic Books, 1981.

3. Sullivan, *The Interpersonal Theory of Psychiatry*.

4. But we can also become "special" by becoming the object of others' projections, that is, a scapegoat.

5. This phenomenon occurs in many different types of groups, not just the workplace. The scapegoat may even be subtly encouraged or "cued" to speak the "truth" that others fear to say. We discuss this more completely in chapter 7.

6. The literature in family therapy, especially the work of Carl Whitaker describes this process eloquently. So does the Jungian analyst Sylvia Brinton Perera in her book *The Scapegoat Complex: Toward a Mythology of Shadow and Guilt*, Inner City Books, 1986. Perera is particularly concerned with the ways that scapegoating represents an internalized transpersonal process, but she has this to say about the familial origins of the scapegoat: "The adult scapegoat's inability to develop a personal identity and self-confidence is due to having been burdened very early in life with those elements devalued, denied, repressed and dissociated by the parents, who initially represent the collective" (p. 30).

7. S. Fraiberg, *The Magic Years*, Scribner, 1959.

8. Jean Piaget and B. Inhelder, *The Psychology of the Child*, Basic Books, 1969.

9. This principle that "the map is not the territory, and the name is not the thing named" was articulated by Alfred Korzybski and is discussed extensively by Gregory Bateson in *Mind and Nature*, Bantam, 1969.

10. A fascinating though exceptional instance of this process was reported by M.S. Gazzaniga and J.E. LeDoux in *The Integrated Mind*, Plenum, 1978. They studied individuals who had a "split-brain," that is, the communications links between the two hemispheres had been severed in an attempt to stop the sympathetic spread of epileptic lesions. When asked to explain their response to a task assigned to the right hemisphere, the left hemisphere (which controls speech) would respond with plausible but entirely nonfactual stories about the acts of the other hemisphere.

11. L. Klepp, "Speak of the Devil," *Mirabella* (April 1995): 79–80.

12. Carl Jung was perhaps the foremost exponent of the necessity of

attending to unconscious process. For Jung the unconscious holds the key to spiritual as well as emotional development (see especially *Memories, Dreams, Reflections*, Vintage Books, 1961).

When unconscious motivation—especially unconscious conflict—is ignored, psychotherapists may find themselves in the stance of trying to argue their patients out of their symptoms. Sometimes this works. Sometimes it only drives the problem deeper, or drives the patient away.

When conscious considerations of efficiency rule therapy, unconscious ideas appear to fade. Their residue can sometimes be felt as whispering, unvoiced bodily sensations, and in the archaic language of what Sullivan called the "uncanny" affect, including dread, awe, and disgust.

If, in the name of efficiency, we impose rationality as the only valid voice in the therapy, we run the risk of becoming tyrants—not only to our patients, but also to ourselves. We begin to lose tolerance for human frailty. If we are already top-heavy in the superego department, we will be judgmental toward others and merciless to ourselves, inviting withdrawal and depression, if not worse.

13. M. Feffer, "Symptom Expression as a Form of Primitive Decentering," *Psychological Review* 32 (1967): 434–44.

14. Terence was the son of a Libyan slave who became a respected writer. He lived from about 185 to 159 B.C.E. The quotation is from his *Heauton Timorumenos*, 77. The complete citation is *"Homo sum; humani nil a me alienum puto."*

15. Relational templates resemble what Jungian psychologists call archetypes. We find it useful to always focus on an archetype as a pattern that connects, even when this connection seems destructive. For example, if we think of the hero, we must also think of the villain. If we remember that both exist in each party to the drama, that is, the hero is also a villain and the villain also a hero, we are less vulnerable to projection.

16. See R. Forero, L. McLellan, C. Risel, and A. Bauman, "Bullying Behaviour and Psychosocial Health among School Students in New South Wales, Australia: Cross Sectional Survey," *British Medical Journal* 319 (August 1999), and, in that same issue, R. Kaltiala-Heino, M. Rimpela, M. Marttunen, A. Rimpela, and P. Rantanen, "Bullying, Depression, and Suicidal Ideation in Finnish Adolescents: School Survey."

17. J. Loevinger, "The Meaning and Measurement of Ego Development," *American Psychologist* 27 (1966): 195–206.

18. The reader may object here that bullying is different from scapegoating since bullying tends to be one individual attacking another, and we are emphasizing the systemic nature of scapegoating. We believe, however, that there are important similarities: a victim is singled out (identified), stigmatized (as weak, sissy, etc.) with the projections of the bully,

and isolated (banished) by being repeatedly shamed in front of others. Although there are various motives for bullying, it provides an important emotional and relational template for later experience. We also believe that the most effective interventions are systemic, that is, reducing the social acceptability of bullying. Recently the topic of workplace bullying has received more attention in both the professional and popular press. See for example, C. Alderman, "Bullying in the Workplace: A Survey," *Nursing Standards* 11, no. 35 (May 2, 1997): 22–24; and G. Namie and R. Namie, *Bully Proof Yourself at Work*, Patson's Press, 1999.

19. See C. Salmivalli, "Participant Role Approach to School Bullying: Implications for Interventions," *Journal of Adolescents* 22, no. 4 (August 1999): 453–59; and in the same issue, P. O'Connell, D. Pepler, and W. Craig, "Peer Involvement in Bullying: Insights and Challenges for Intervention," 437–52.

20. Another way of viewing this relation is to examine how both roles define each other. It is challenging to hold both poles of an archetype simultaneously—to see yourself as both oppressor and oppressed, as angel and devil at once. Taoism and Buddhism are much more at home with this ambiguity. The Taoist notion of the Taiji, the circle divided into Yin and Yang, light and dark, and the Buddhist admonition against judging "good" and "evil" allow consideration of the ways that each pole of the archetype supports and defines the other. In this view each is necessary for the existence of the other, and the "truth," as much as it can be expressed, is "both/and" rather than "either/or." Many of the martial arts look at how the opponent is contained within and how the target is already implicit in the act of aiming the bow.

21. Hidetaka Abe, personal communication (conversation) 1984.

CHAPTER 5

1. See R. Girard, *The Scapegoat*, Johns Hopkins University Press, 1986, for a critique of early writers (such as Frazer) and contemporary scholars (such as Lévi-Strauss).

2. Interestingly, there are anecdotal reports that some of the "dot-com startup" companies, while extremely tolerant of casual dress and flexible working hours, are relatively suspicious of older workers. One can speculate that since most of the owners of these companies are young, they are forming their corporate culture by differentiating themselves generationally. That is, they are creating group cohesion by the relative homogeneity of the age of their workers.

3. BOAC Captain Neil Johnston discusses the negative relation between blame and punishment and understanding aircraft mishaps in a

series on "organizational risk management," which can be found on the Internet at http://www.natcavoice.org/av/avs/punish.htm, originally published in *British Fight Deck* 15 (1995).

4. Michael Lerner coined this term. He applies it to many organizational and political situations. See especially his book, *Surplus Powerlessness—The Psychodynamics of Everyday Life and the Psychology of Individual and Social Transformation*, Prometheus Books, 1991.

5. See L. Festinger, *A Theory of Cognitive Dissonance*, Row, Peterson, 1957. While this effect can be demonstrated consistently in the laboratory, there is some disagreement between researchers on its importance in common life situations. See also R. Brown, *Social Psychology*, Free Press, 1965.

6. We see this particularly among the professionals whom we have worked with. That is, being used to status, privilege, and a good deal of freedom in their work, they tend to adopt individual strategies to solving problems at work and seem especially invested in believing that managerial criticism of a colleague must have been deserved. It is an affront to their sense of autonomy to believe that workplace success may be capricious or arbitrary.

7. See Girard, *The Scapegoat*.

8. A dramatic historical example of this is the "Loyalty Oath" controversy at the University of California in the mid-1950s. Faculty were asked to sign an oath of loyalty to the United States. Many faculty, including some who were decorated veterans of the military, refused on principle. They were accused of being "communists" and "disloyal" and were persecuted and threatened with the loss of their jobs.

9. This cycle is known as "deviation amplifying feedback." It is a process that most of us know from listening to a public address system screech. It is also a useful way to model many interpersonal and emotional phenomena. For a practical application of this model, see J. Dyckman, "A Communications Model of Panic Disorder," *Anxiety Disorders Practice Journal* 1, no. 2 (1994): 77–82.

CHAPTER 6

1. Blaming the victim is a secondary form of scapegoating. It is once removed from the actual victimization, but compounds the poor treatment the victim has received by again making the victim "other." Victims are distinguished from "normals" by their inability to avoid their victimization. We can speculate that this tendency to blame is itself a measure of the intolerable anxiety aroused in the blamer observing the victim's plight. The observer needs to separate from the victim, and does so by

seeing the victim as somehow "different" from him/herself. If instead we see our own face in the face of the suffering victim, our attitude is likely to change. This is the admonition for compassion that is taught by most religious traditions.

2. D. Schwartz, K. Dodge, G. Petit, and J. Bates, "The Early Socialization of Aggressive Victims of Bullying," *Child Development* 68, no. 4 (August 1997): 665–75.

3. A. Zaleznik, "The Dynamics of Subordinacy," in "How Successful Executives Handle People," *Harvard Business Review*, Studies on Communication and Management Skills (1970): 142.

4. P. Frost and S. Robinson, "The Toxic Handler: Organizational Hero—and Casualty," *Harvard Business Review* (July–August 1999): 97–106.

5. The Japanese have coined the term *Karoshi* to describe "death from overwork"—literally dying on the job. This is a term of both pride and caution as the society expects workers to dedicate themselves to their workplaces at the expense of their other commitments and even their own health.

6. See especially the family therapy of Carl Whitaker. A good introduction to the breadth of his work is found in *From Psyche to System: The Evolving Therapy of Carl Whitaker*, ed. J.R. Neill and D.P. Kniskern, Guilford Press, 1982.

7. We have seen this pattern repeatedly in individuals who present to psychiatry clinics for "job stress." The organizational cultures of some companies seem to promote or ignore dysfunctional managers. We have noticed this especially in the U.S. Postal Service. We speculate that the tendency of the Postal Service to hire military veterans may inadvertently contribute to a culture in which managers feel free to exercise their authority capriciously and expect immediate obedience to patently unfair "orders." The mixture of civilian expectations of "fairness" and military expectations of "obedience" leads to conflict. This climate is ripe for the top dog/underdog scapegoating described in this chapter.

8. For readers interested in Jungian thought, also known as analytical psychology, an excellent beginning can be found in F. Fordham, *An Introduction to Jung's Psychology*, Penguin Books, 1953. Those who prefer original texts might want to start with Jung's lectures to the Tavistock Institute in London, published as *Analytical Psychology: Its Theory and Practice*, Vintage, 1968.

9. Sylvia Perera discusses this in some detail in *The Scapegoat Complex*, Inner City Books, 1986. She points out that many women become "scapegoat-identified" as they participate in the process of blaming themselves. This is easy to do when the predominant messages they receive from the culture devalue aspects of their own personality.

10. See William Bridges, *The Character of Organizations,* Consulting Psychologists Press, Inc., 1992.

11. For many years nurses have been low in status and power but high in responsibility in the medical system. This makes them extremely vulnerable to both blame and anxiety. A news story in the *San Francisco Chronicle,* September 15, 1999, p. A11, illustrates this poignantly. A physician ordered too much of a chemotherapeutic agent, and nurses administered it with fatal consequences for two patients. The nurses faced suspension and loss of their licenses for failing to catch the physician's mistake, even though several had questioned the doctor's orders before finally following them.

CHAPTER 7

1. D. Olewus, "Victimization by Peers: Antecedents and Long-term Out-comes," in *Social Withdrawal, Inhibition, and Shyness in Children,* ed. K.H. Rubin and J.B. Asendorpf, Erlbaum, 1993.

2. Note the implication that you think that a number of different people *should* be told. This is one of the ways you can gently educate your coworkers about the process.

3. Being the first to suggest something new can carry rewards as well as risks. However, if you feel that your workplace culture supports scapegoating, you would do well to remember the words of Machiavelli (see chapter 9), who said, "For the initiator has the enmity of all who would profit by the preservation of the old institutions and merely luke-warm defenders in those who would gain by the new ones." *The Prince,* translated by T. Bergin, Appleton-Century-Crofts, 1947, p. 15.

4. The family therapist Lyman Wynne called this phenomenon the "rubber fence." He was describing something that most family therapists have experienced: even after they have apparently been accepted as part of the family system, if they propose an unacceptable change, they will find themselves rapidly on the outside looking in—as though they were expelled by an invisible elastic boundary.

5. A. Zaleznik, "The Dynamics of Subordinacy," in "How Successful Executives Handle People," *Harvard Business Review,* Studies on Communication and Management Skills (1970): 142.

CHAPTER 8

1. This tendency to "freeze" in the face of danger is a powerful behavioral tendency. It has survival value in some situations; for instance, the frozen deer may become "invisible" to predators who rely on move-

ment to detect their prey. This same behavior, however, leads to disaster for the deer on the highway. Primates show this same tendency to "fight, flight, or freeze" when frightened. We are counting on our executive cortical functions to override our evolutionary first line of defense and to come up with a more complex and successful strategic response.

2. The idea of the "fearless inventory" can be found in *Twelve Steps and Twelve Traditions*, Alcoholics Anonymous World Services.

3. See, for example, the work of Justin Kruger and David Dunning, "Unskilled and Unaware of It: How Difficulties in Recognizing One's Own Incompetence Lead to Inflated Self Assessments," *Journal of Personality and Social Psychology 77*, no. 6 (December 1999): 1121–34.

4. Think about high school biology class and how difficult it was to get a live amoeba to stay in one place long enough to look at it under the microscope. If you used one of the needlelike probes to try to hold it, it just flowed around the probe and out of your range of view. You had to maneuver at least two probes, from different directions, in order to get it to remain roughly in one place. Systems are similar—they tend to "flow around" any attempt to influence them. This tendency to remain the same, whether amoeba or system, is called "homeostasis."

5. This principle of first "joining" with an opponent is highly developed in the martial arts. It has been articulated most clearly in the Japanese martial art Aikido. Founded in the early twentieth century by Morihei Ueshiba, Aikido teaches a discipline of "noncollision" and of joining one's energy or *ki* to the universal. While the philosophy of Aikido is to harmonize and resolve conflicts, it is also an extremely effective and powerful martial art. An excellent introduction can be found in a collection edited by Richard Strozzi Heckler, *Aikido and the New Warrior*, North Atlantic Books, 1985.

6. See J. Pennebaker, *Opening Up: The Healing Power of Expressing Emotions*, Guilford, 1990. There is controversy over why this works. One of the most interesting hypotheses is that social "reality" is a *construction* of brain activity. That is, it does not exist independent of the *thoughts* of the participants. Changing the way we think about a situation not only influences behavior, but also how the behavior of others is interpreted, and most important, how we experience a situation and what emotions arise. In effect, we are always telling ourselves stories about how we are in relation to others. When we make those stories explicit, we create the possibilities to consciously edit and revise our experience. Looking for "positives" in an experience can change the emotional impact of that experience in ways that are beneficial to our psychological and physical health. This does not mean that Pollyanna was absolutely right, but that she was on to something.

7. T.H. Holmes and R.H. Rahe pioneered this with their studies of the relation between major life changes and likelihood of hospitalization. They found that the sum of numeric scores of life changes (including "good" events like getting married or falling in love) in one year was highly predictive of hospitalization in the subsequent year. See their paper, "The Social Readjustment Rating Scale," *Journal of Psychosomatic Research* 11 (1967): 213–18. This fits with the earlier work of Hans Selye who defined stress as the body's "nonspecific reaction to change." See Hans Selye, *The Stress of Life*, McGraw-Hill, 1956.

8. The pioneering work was done by M. Seligman and is summarized his book *Helplessness*, Freeman, 1997.

9. Large corporations have taken to hiring anthropologists to observe CEOs' behavior during their workdays. Because they are trained to see the hidden rules of "culture," anthropologists can give useful feedback to the CEOs about the impact of their behavior on the functioning of the workplace.

Psychotherapists have long noticed the difference in hearing about a marital problem from one of the members in individual therapy and observing the problem directly when the couple is present for marital therapy. This has led systems thinkers to claim that the "truth" of a system can be seen only when all members are present.

CHAPTER 9

1. Niccolo Machiavelli, *The Prince*, translated by Thomas Bergin, Appleton-Century-Crofts, 1947, p. 44.

2. Ibid., p. 70.

3. D. Goleman, *Working with Emotional Intelligence*, Bantam Books, 1988.

4. The developmental events that leave individuals particularly vulnerable to the pain of empathic failure and the ways that they can recover are dealt with in a brilliant, but difficult to read, fashion by Heinz Kohut. See particularly H. Kohut, *The Analysis of the Self*, International University Press, 1971. Kohut called this process of empathic understanding of the empathic failure "transmuting internalization," p. 40.

5. Machiavelli, *The Prince*, p. 6.

6. Ibid., p. 52.

7. Personalities do come into play by increasing the likelihood that we will fall into or "adopt" different roles. For example, the conscientious and even "righteous" individual is more likely to become an "idealist" scapegoat than is a gregarious, self-protective extrovert.

8. Machiavelli, *The Prince*, p. xiii.

9. Machiavelli spends *a lot* of his book relating the military and political history of ancient Rome and Greece, but he also finds ample parallels in the wars and turmoils of the Italian peninsula at the time of his writing.

10. There is a relevant Zulu proverb: "Until the lion learns to speak, the story of the hunt will always favor the hunters."

11. Machiavelli, *The Prince*, p. 48.

12. Even though we now have sophisticated electronic GPS (global positioning satellites), the principle is the same: comparing information from two distinct sources. In GPS, a radio signal is sent simultaneously from two different satellites, and the time difference between the receiver and the source signals allows calculation of position of the receiver to remarkably small tolerances (within a meter).

13. T.E. Deal and A.A. Kennedy, *Corporate Cultures—The Rites and Rituals of Corporate Life*, Addison Wesley, 1982, p. 85.

14. Machiavelli, *The Prince*, pp. 50–51.

15. Ibid., p. 29.

16. Ibid., p. 31.

17. A good model of how to do this can be found in the magazine *Nursing* 99 (August 1999): 54–56. See also the Web site, http://www.springnet.com.

18. Machiavelli, *The Prince*, p. 53.

19. This kind of implicit message about the relationship is called a "meta-message." Meta-messages qualify the content of a message and help to define the relationship between the persons sending and receiving the message. Every message proposes a relationship between people. Tone, prosody, and social convention are present in every utterance and make each act of speech a multilayered event of meaning. For instance, if a casual acquaintance asks, "How are you?" the expected answer may be formulaic and relatively impersonal: "Fine." But if a friend asks in a solicitous tone, "How *are* you?" you might really want to tell the questioner in detail, and expect that s/he would listen attentively! If the acquaintance asks, "How are you?" the question can feel like an attempt to redefine the relationship, which may or may not be welcome. Paul Watzlawick, Janet Beavin, and Don Jackson explored the intricacies of meta-messages in their classic book *The Pragmatics of Human Communication*, W.W. Norton, 1967.

20. Machiavelli, *The Prince*, p. 72.

CHAPTER 10

1. It was not long ago in European history that occupation and identity were even more closely entwined. Think about the number of people

you know whose surname is an occupation. Many are obvious, such as Miller, Baker, or Smith. Others represent occupations that are now extinct or rare, such as Chandler (made light fixtures), Fletcher (feathered arrows), Cooper (made barrels), or Wheelwright.

2. Psychologist James Averill speculates that the experience of grief has evolved as a social emotion that makes separation from the group extremely punishing. While grief may not be so good for the individual in this view, it would have some evolutionary benefit for the *group* by increasing cohesiveness (since no one enjoys grief) and hence the likelihood of group survival. His argument is set out in more detail in his article, "Grief: Its Nature and Significance," *Psychological Bulletin* 70, no. 6 (1968): 721–48.

Another psychologist, Nathan Adler, pointed out that a funeral not only honors the dead but also serves as a ritual to validate the mourners' new identity and status. It is a way of reestablishing the community or group after the loss of a member by reassuring the mourners that they still have a place. Adler noted that many systems of "conduct reorganization," including religious conversion rituals, some psychotherapies (some charismatic group drug or alcohol programs), and coercive prisoner-of-war brainwashing, make deliberate use of the death/rebirth theme in altering a person's identification with his/her social reference group. See T. Sarbin and N. Adler's paper, "Communalities in Systems of Conduct Reorganization," presented at the California State Psychological Association, San Diego, CA, January 1967.

3. Freud first hypothesized guilt as one of the factors that differentiates normal grief from pathological sadness in "Mourning and Melancholia," originally published in 1917. In J. Strachey, ed., *The Standard Edition of the Complete Psychological Works of Sigmund Freud*, Vol. 14, Hogarth, 1957.

4. For up-to-date statistics on the incidence and prevalence of depression, consult the NIMH Web site at http://www.nimh.nih.gov.

5. The interaction between emotions and the functioning of the immune system has been found to be more extensive and more complex than previously thought. Emotions can help or hinder immune function, and chemicals produced by the immune system can profoundly alter moods. See C.B. Nemeroff, "The Neurobiology of Depression," *Scientific American* 278 (1998): 42–49.

6. The Beck Depression Inventory is a proprietary measure that has been employed in numerous studies of depression and its treatment. It has the advantage of being "normed"—that is, of being able to compare a subject's answers with the answers of many others suffering depression, and so to be able to give a quantitative estimate of the severity of the depression.

7. There is evidence that exposure to extreme stress, including major depressive episodes, alters sensitivity to future stressors. That is, it takes less stress to precipitate another episode. See T.L. Holbrook, J.P. Anderson, W.J. Sieber, D. Browner, and D.B. Hoyt, "Outcome after Major Trauma: Discharge and 6-Month Follow-up Results from the Trauma Recovery Project," *Journal of Trauma: Injury, Infection, and Critical Care* 45, no. 2 (1998): 315–24; and also K.S. Kendler, L.M. Thornton, and C.O. Gardner, "Stressful Life Events and Previous Episodes in the Etiology of Major Depression in Women: An Evaluation of the 'Kindling' Hypothesis," *American Journal of Psychiatry* 157, no. 8 (2000): 1243–51.

8. The July/August 1996 issue of *Family Therapy Networker* is devoted to a series of articles on the biology and treatment of PTSD. While relatively ignored in the public literature until the post-Vietnam era, there are now several journals that deal specifically with the impact of trauma and the ways it can be ameliorated.

9. The literature on the psychological effects of exercise is nicely reviewed by P. Salmon, "Effects of Physical Exercise on Anxiety, Depression, and Sensitivity to Stress: A Unifying Theory." *Clinical Psychology Review* 21, no. 1 (February 2001): 33–61.

Animal studies have shown that exercise increases brain-derived neurotrophic factor messenger RNA levels in the hippocampus. Giving antidepressant medicines also increases these levels. While this does not prove that antidepressants and exercise are equivalent, it is intriguing and suggests that they may share a common pathway to lifting depression. See A.A. Russo-Neustadt, R.C. Beard, Y.M. Huang, and C.W. Cotman, "Physical Activity and Anti-depressant Treatment Potentiate the Expression of Specific Brain-Derived Neurotrophic Factor Transcripts in the Rat Hippocampus," *Neuroscience* 101, no. 2 (2000): 305–12.

There is controversy over the strength of the effects of physical exercise on depression. Most of the research has been with mildly depressed persons, and it seems clear that moderate exercise two or three times a week does help lift depression and enhance well-being. It is not as clear that exercise will benefit severely depressed persons, but studies are complicated by the difficulty in getting more severely depressed persons to engage in the treatment, that is, to get out and exercise.

However, one very recent study has shown a surprising finding. It compared three groups of patients who met the criteria for major depression. One group was treated with an antidepressant medicine that is widely used and effective, a second received medicine and aerobic exercise, while the third did exercise alone. At the end of four months, all three groups showed about the same rates of significant improvement—their moods and symptoms no longer met the criteria for major depressive disorder. At a ten-month follow-up, the group that did exercise alone had the *lowest* rate of relapse. This suggests that a change in lifestyle—namely, increased regular exercise—helps protect against depression making a "comeback." See M. Bayak et al., "Exercise Treatment for Major Depression: Maintenance of Therapeutic Benefit at 10 Months," *Psychosomatic Medicine* 62 (2000): 633–38.

But perhaps the most intriguing finding is that patients in the exercise alone group did better than those in the exercise plus medication group. The authors speculate that patients in the exercise alone group attributed their improvement to their own activity, thus increasing their sense of mastery and positive self-regard. The patients in the exercise plus medication group were more likely to credit the medicine, although some expressed negative attitudes about psychiatric medication. This raises important issues about how attitude and attributional factors relate to therapeutic success.

10. Carbohydrate craving seems to accompany depression, especially in women. See J.D. Carter, P.R. Joyce, R.T. Mulder, S.E. Luty, and J. McKenzie, "Gender Differences in the Presentation of Depressed Outpatients: A Comparison of Descriptive Variables," *Journal of Affective Disorders* 61, no. 1–2 (December 2000): 59–67.

One theory suggests that depression is due to a lack of the neurotransmitter serotonin and that carbohydrate-rich snacks temporarily restore serotonergic transmission and lessen depressive symptoms. However, this effect appears to be small and of little therapeutic value. See A.C. Toornvliet et al., "Psychological and Metabolic Responses of Carbohydrate Craving Obese Patients to Carbohydrate, Fat and Protein-Rich Meals," *International Journal Obesity Related Metabolic Disorders* 21, no. 10 (October 1997): 860–64.

11. The work of Aaron Beck has been the most influential in launching the movement called "cognitive therapy." Beck, a clinical psychologist who had been trained in psychoanalytic theory, noted that his patients often had rapid, telegraphic, and automatic thoughts that cued their emotional state. Often these thoughts were illogical and distorted, but they set off strong feelings of anxiety or depression. Beck found that if these thoughts were brought into awareness and consciously challenged, the feelings changed. A description of his pioneering work can be found in his book, *Cognitive Therapy and the Emotional Disorders*, International Universities Press, 1976. A number of others have built on his work, especially on the influence of thought on depression. An excellent self-help book is David Burns's *Feeling Good: The New Mood Therapy*, Avon, 1999.

12. From a developmental perspective (see chapter 4), we can say that

exposure plus caring is equivalent to the experience of being *held and seen*, both of which are crucial processes in the child's development of a sense of self as a whole person, that is, as a person who has complex, and sometimes contradictory feelings, and who may have thoughts that would be socially unacceptable if they were translated to overt behavior. But even so, the child is seen as "okay"—an acceptable member of the group.

13. Noticing how automatic thoughts trigger changes in mood is itself a useful and important insight. We are constantly commenting to ourselves about the state of the world and our relation to it. Often we are giving ourselves incomplete and frequently inaccurate information. Learning to question our internal commentary is part of "waking" from a state of self-delusion—a process that has been advocated by religious traditions for at least 2,500 years.

14. Steve Kettmann, "Barry Bonds' Talk Delights Little Leaguers," *San Francisco Chronicle*, Monday, May 24, 1993.

CHAPTER 11

1. The "fall-guy/gal" and "top dog/underdog" scapegoat types are the least likely to have identified with the role of scapegoat and are hence most likely to experience the attack as coming from the "outside." The "redeemer" and the "shadow" types may experience scapegoating as another chapter or scene in a familiar drama and are often more likely to join with their accuser in believing that somehow they are, in fact, at fault or bad. Since the accusation joins their own unconscious accusation of themselves, they tend not to locate the source of attack as "harassment."

2. From Joseph A. Kinney, *Violence at Work*, Prentice Hall, 1995, p. 14.

3. Paul Hawkin, *Growing a Business*, Simon & Schuster, 1987, p. 218.

4. Paul Hawkin, *The Ecology of Commerce: A Declaration of Sustainability*, Harper Business, 1994.

5. Personal communication.

6. A. Bandura and R. Walters, *Social Learning and Personality Development*, Holt, Rinehart and Winston, 1964.

7. See, for example, one of the textbooks in organizational development, W. Rothwell, R. Sullivan, and G. McLean, eds., *Practicing Organizational Development: A Guide for Consultants*, Pfeiffer & Co., 1995, p. 315.

8. Hawkin, *Growing a Business*, p. 216.

9. Lani Guinier, Michelle Fine, and Jane Balin, *Becoming Gentlemen*, Beacon Press, 1997, p. 4.

10. C.G. Jung, *Analytic Psychology: Its Theory and Practice*, Vintage Books, 1968, p. 22.

11. See Jay Haley, *Strategies of Psychotherapy*, Grune & Stratton, 1963. Another way of looking at this connection is found in the work of the business executive Max DePree, who wrote, "Opportunity must always be connected to accountability. This is not something hopelessly idealistic. Without the promise of accountability, there are no true opportunities and risks. Without true opportunity and risk, there is no chance to seize accountability; it will remain elsewhere." *Leadership Is an Art*, Dell, 1989, p. 145.

12. James Hollis, *The Middle Passage: From Misery to Meaning in Midlife*, Inner City Books, 1993, p. 34.

13. The Italian psychiatrist Gianfranco Cecchin advocates "curiosity" as an alternative to judging. Curiosity maintains the "unfinished" quality of perception. This allows us to tolerate ambiguity and to permit revision of our opinion. More of his work can be found in "Hypothesizing, Circularity, and Neutrality Revisited: An Invitation to Curiosity," *Family Process* 26, no. 4 (1987): 405–13.

This "curiosity" is very like the "investigative" attitude cultivated by mindfulness meditation (Vipassana) practice. By focusing on the specific sensations of experience, we begin to dissolve (or "deconstruct") the automatic "stories" that we have constructed about our reality. This allows the practitioner to experience reality in a fresher, more fluid, complex, and full fashion.

14. P. Senge and M. Wheatley, "Changing How We Work Together," *Shambala Sun* (January 2001): 33.

15. John Stuart Mill, *Utilitarianism, Liberty, and Representative Government*, Dutton & Co., 1940 (originally 1859).

16. "Four Days with W. Edwards Deming," an unattributed article published by the W. Edwards Deming Institute, www.deming.org/theman/articles_fourdays02.html.

17. Angeles Arrien, "Action Principles of Deep Engagement" *The Institute of Noetic Sciences Membership Booklet*, Author, 2000, p. 20. Arrien has also edited *Working Together: Producing Synergy by Honoring Diversity*, Benett-Koehler, 2001, which develops this theme in more detail.

18. I. Myers, *Introduction to Type*, Consulting Psychologists Press, 1987.

19. For examples of how this plays out in the workplace, see M. Stein and J. Hollwitz, eds., *Psyche at Work*, Chiron Publications, 1992.

20. BOAC Captain Neil Johnston, "Do Blame and Punishment Have a Role in Organizational Risk Management?" *British Flight Deck* 15 (spring 1995), also available on the Web at www.natcavoice.org/av/avs/punish.htm.

21. DePree, *Leadership Is an Art*, p. 145.

22. W. Edwards Deming, *Out of the Crisis*, MIT Press, 1986.

23. John P. Fernandez has developed this theme in a number of his works. It is powerfully stated in *Diversity Advantage: How American Business Can Out-Perform Japanese and European Companies in the Global Marketplace*, Jossey-Bass, 1993.

Bibliography

Alderman, C. "Bullying in the Workplace: A Survey." *Nursing Standards* 11, no. 35 (May 21, 1997): 22–24.

Altman, I. *The Environment and Social Behavior.* Brooks/Cole, 1975.

Arrien, A. "Action Principles of Deep Engagement." *Institute of Noetic Sciences Membership Booklet,* 2000.

Arrien, A., ed. *Working Together: Producing Synergy by Honoring Diversity.* Benett-Koehler, 2000.

Asch, S. "Studies of Independence and Conformity." *Psychological Monographs* 70 (9 Whole No. 416), 1956.

Averill, J. "Grief: Its Nature and Significance." *Psychological Bulletin* 70, no. 6 (1968): 721–48.

Bakan, D. *Disease, Pain & Sacrifice.* Beacon Press, 1968.

Bandura, A., and R. Walters. *Social Learning and Personality Development.* Holt, Rhinehart and Winston, 1963.

Bateson, G. *Steps to an Ecology of Mind.* Ballantine, 1972.

Bateson, G. *Mind and Nature.* Bantam, 1979.

Bayak, M., et al. "Exercise Treatment for Major Depression: Maintenance of Therapeutic Benefit at 10 Months." *Psychosomatic Medicine* 62 (2000): 633–38.

Beck, A. *Cognitive Therapy and the Emotional Disorders.* International Universities Press, 1976.

Bion, W. *Experiences in Groups.* Basic Books, 1961.

Bowlby, J. *Attachment and Loss:* Vol. 3, *Loss: Sadness and Depression.* Basic Books, 1980.

Bridges, W. *The Character of Organizations.* Consulting Psychologists Press, Inc., 1992.

Brown, R. *Social Psychology.* Free Press, 1965.

Bulman, R. Analysis: "Blaming Ex-leaders Is Popular in S. Korea." *Reuters News Service*, July 11, 1998.

Burns, D. *Feeling Good: The New Mood Therapy*. Avon, 1999.

Calhoun, J.B. "A Behavioral Sink." In *Roots of Behavior*, edited by E.L. Bliss. Harper & Row, 1962.

Carter, J.D., P.R. Joyce, R.T. Mulder, S.E. Luty, and J. McKenzie. "Gender Differences in the Presentation of Depressed Outpatients: A Comparison of Descriptive Variables." *Journal of Affective Disorders* 61, no. 1–2 (December 2000): 59–67.

Cecchin, G. "Hypothesizing, Circularity, and Neutrality Revisited: An Invitation to Curiosity." *Family Process* 26, no. 4 (1987): 405–13.

Deal, T.E., and A.A. Kennedy. *Corporate Cultures—The Rites and Rituals of Corporate Life*. Addison Wesley, 1982.

Deming, W.E. *Out of the Crisis*. MIT Press, 1986.

DePree, M. *Leadership Is an Art*. Dell, 1989.

Dyckman, J. "A Communications Model of Panic Disorder." *Anxiety Disorders Practice Journal* 1, no. 2 (1994): 77–82.

Family Therapy Networker (July/August 1996).

Feffer, M. "Symptom Expression as a Form of Primitive Decentering." *Psychological Review* 32 (1967): 434–41.

Fernandez, J.P. *Diversity Advantage: How American Business Can Out-Perform Japanese and European Companies in the Global Marketplace*. Jossey-Bass, 1993.

Festinger, L. *A Theory of Cognitive Dissonance*. Row, Peterson, 1957.

Fordham, F. *An Introduction to Jung's Psychology*. Penguin Books, 1953.

Forero, R., L. McLellan, C. Risel, and A. Bauman. "Bullying Behaviour and Psychosocial Health among School Students in New South Wales, Australia: Cross Sectional Survey." *British Medical Journal* 319 (1999): 344–48.

"Four Days with W. Edwards Deming." The W. Edwards Deming Institute. n.d., Available at: www.deming.org/theman/articles/articlrs_fourdays02.html.

Fraiberg, S. *The Magic Years*. Scribner, 1959.

Frazer, James. *The Golden Bough*. Wordsworth, 1993. (Original work published in 1922.)

Freud, S. *Moses & Monotheism*. Standard Edition 23. New York, 1939.

Freud, S. "Mourning and Melancholia." In *The Standard Edition of the Complete Psychological Works of Sigmund Freud*, edited by J. Strachey, Vol. 14. Hogarth, 1957. (Original work published in 1917.)

Frost, P., and S. Robinson. "The Toxic Handler: Organizational Hero—and Casualty." *Harvard Business Review* (July–August 1999): 97–106.

Gaster, T. *Myth, Legend and Custom in the Old Testament*, Harper & Row, 1969.

Gazzaniga, M.S., and J.E. Le Doux. *The Integrated Mind*. Plenum, 1978.

Girard, R. *The Scapegoat*. Johns Hopkins University Press, 1986.

Goleman, D. *Working with Emotional Intelligence*. Bantam Books, 1998.

Guinier, L., M. Fine, and J. Balin. *Becoming Gentlemen*. Beacon Press, 1997.

Haley, J. *Strategies of Psychotherapy*. Grune & Stratton, 1963.

Haney, C., W.C. Banks, and P.G. Zimbardo "Interpersonal Dynamics in a Simulated Prison." *International Journal of Criminology and Penology* 1 (1973): 69–97.

Haney, C., and P.G. Zimbardo. "The Past and Future of U.S. Prison Policy: Twenty-five Years after the Stanford Prison Experiment." *American Psychologist* 53 (1998): 709–27.

Hawkin, P. *Growing a Business*. Simon & Schuster, 1987.

Hawkin, P. *The Ecology of Commerce: A Declaration of Sustainability*. Harper Business, 1994.

Heckler, R.S., ed. *Aikido and the New Warrior*. North Atlantic Books, 1985.

Holbrook, T.L., J.P. Anderson, W.J. Sieber, D. Browner, and D.B. Hoyt. "Outcome after Major Trauma: Discharge and 6-Month Follow-up Results from the Trauma Recovery Project." *Journal of Trauma: Injury, Infection, and Critical Care* 45, no. 2 (1998): 315–24.

Hollis, J. *The Middle Passage: From Misery to Meaning in Midlife*. Inner City Books, 1993.

Holmes, T.H., and R.H. Rahe. "The Social Readjustment Rating Scale." *Journal of Psychosomatic Research* 11 (1967): 213–18.

Jaynes, J. *The Origins of Consciousness and the Breakdown of the Bicameral Mind*. Houghton-Mifflin, 1976.

Johnston, N. "Do Blame and Punishment Have a Role in Organizational Risk Management?" *British Flight Deck* 15 (spring 1995).

Jung, C.G. *Memories, Dreams, Reflections*. Vintage Books, 1961.

Jung, C.G. *Analytical Psychology: Its Theory & Practice*. Vintage Books, 1968.

Kaltiala-Heino, R., M. Rimpela, M. Marttunen, A. Rimpela, and P. Rantanen. "Bullying, Depression, and Suicidal Ideation in Finnish Adolescents: School Survey." *British Medical Journal* 319 (1999): 348–51.

Kendler, K.S., L.M. Thornton, and C.O. Gardner. "Stressful Life Events and Previous Episodes in the Etiology of Major Depression in Women: An Evaluation of the 'Kindling' Hypothesis." *American Journal of Psychiatry* 157, no. 8 (2000): 1243–51.

Kettmann, S. "Barry Bonds' Talk Delights Little Leaguers." *San Francisco Chronicle*, May 24, 1993.

Kinney, J.A. *Violence at Work*. Prentice Hall, 1995.

Klaus, M.H., and Kennell, J.H. *Parent-Infant Bonding*. Mosby, 1982.

Klepp, L. "Speak of the Devil." *Mirabella* (April 1995): 79–80.

Kohut, H. *The Analysis of the Self*. International University Press, Inc., 1971.

Kruger, J., and D. Dunning. "Unskilled and Unaware of It: How Difficulties in Recognizing One's Own Incompetence Lead to Inflated Self Assessments." *Journal of Personality and Social Psychology 77*, no. 6 (1999): 1121–34.

Lacan, J. *The Four Fundamental Concepts of Psychoanalysis*. W.W. Norton, 1973.

Lerner, M. *Surplus Powerlessness—The Psychodynamics of Everyday Life and the Psychology of Individual and Social Transformation*. Prometheus Books, 1991.

Liddel, H.G., and Scott, R. *Greek-English Lexicon*, 7th ed. Clarendon Press, 1997.

Loevinger, J. "The Meaning and Measurement of Ego Development." *American Psychologist* 21 (1966): 195–206.

Machiavelli, N. *The Prince*. Translated by T. Bergin, Appleton-Century-Crofts, 1947.

Malcus, L. "In the Beginning: Biblical and Psychodynamic Bases of Scapegoating." Paper presented at the 55th Annual Conference of the American Group Psychotherapy Association, Chicago, IL, 1998.

Milgram, S. *Obedience to Authority*. Harper & Row, 1974.

Mill, J.S. *Utilitarianism, Liberty, and Representative Government*. Dutton & Co., 1940. (Original work published in 1859.)

Miller, A. *The Drama of the Gifted Child*. Basic Books, 1981.

Myers, I. *Introduction to Type*. Consulting Psychologists Press, 1987.

Namie, G., and R. Namie. *Bully Proof Yourself at Work*. Patson's Press, 1999.

Neill, J.R., and D.P. Kniskern, eds. *From Psyche to System: The Evolving Therapy of Carl Whitaker*. Guilford Press, 1982.

Nemeroff, C.B. "The Neurobiology of Depression." *Scientific American* 278 (1998): 42–49.

Northwestern National Life Insurance Company. "Employee Burnout: America's Newest Epidemic." Minneapolis, MN: Author, 1991.

Nursing 99 (August 1999): 54–56. See also http://www.springnet.com.

O'Connell, P., D. Pepler, and W. Craig. "Peer Involvement in Bullying: Insights and Challenges for Intervention." *Journal of Adolescents* 22, no. 4 (1999): 437–59.

Olewus, D. "Victimization by Peers: Antecedents and Long-term Outcomes." In *Social Withdrawal, Inhibition, and Shyness in Children*, edited by K.H. Rubin and J.B. Asendorpf. Erlbaum, 1993.

Pennebaker, J. *Opening Up: The Healing Power of Expressing Emotions.* Guilford, 1990.

Perera, S.B. *The Scapegoat Complex: Toward a Mythology of Shadow and Guilt.* Inner City Books, 1986.

Piaget, J., and B. Inhelder. *The Psychology of the Child.* Basic Books, 1969.

Princeton Survey Research Associates. "Labor Day Survey: State of Workers." Princeton, NJ: Author, 1997.

Rothwell, W., R. Sullivan, and G. McLean, eds. *Practicing Organizational Development: A Guide for Consultants.* Pfeiffer & Co., 1995.

"Ruling Outrages Nurses." *San Francisco Chronicle*, September 15, 1999, p. A11.

Russo-Neustadt, A.A., R.C. Beard, Y.M. Huang, and C.W. Cotman. "Physical Activity and Anti-depressant Treatment Potentiate the Expression of Specific Brain-Derived Neurotrophic Factor Transcripts in the Rat Hippocampus." *Neuroscience* 101, no. 2 (2000): 305–12.

Salmivalli, C. "Participant Role Approach to School Bullying: Implications for Interventions." *Journal of Adolescents* 22, no. 4 (1999): 453–59.

Salmon, P. "Effects of Physical Exercise on Anxiety, Depression, and Sensitivity to Stress: A Unifying Theory." *Clinical Psychology Review* 21, no. 1 (February 2001): 33–61.

Sapolsky, R. *Why Zebras Don't Get Ulcers.* W.H. Freeman, 1998.

Sarbin, T., and N. Adler. "Communalities in Systems of Conduct Reorganization." Paper presented at the California State Psychological Association, San Diego, CA, January 1967.

Schwartz, D., K. Dodge, G. Petit, and J. Bates. "The Early Socialization of Aggressive Victims of Bullying." *Child Development* 68, no. 4 (August 1997): 665–75.

Seligman, M. *Helplessness.* W.H. Freeman, 1997.

Selye, H. *The Stress of Life.* McGraw-Hill, 1956.

Senege, P., and M. Wheatley. "Changing How We Work Together." *Shambala Sun*, 2001, p. 33.

Sherif, M., O. Harvey, B. White, and W. Hood. *Intergroup Conflict and Cooperation: The Robbers Cave Experiment.* Institute of Group Relations, University of Oklahoma, 1961.

Stein, M., and J. Hollwitz, eds. *Psyche at Work.* Chiron Publications, 1992.

Sullivan, H.S. *The Interpersonal Theory of Psychiatry.* W.W. Norton, 1953.

Toornvliet, A.C. et al. "Psychological and Metabolic Responses of Carbo-
    hydrate Craving Obese Patients to Carbohydrate, Fat and Protein-
    Rich Meals." *International Journal Obesity Related Metabolic Dis-
    orders* 21, no. 10 (October 1997): 860–64.

Twelve Steps and Twelve Traditions. Alcoholics Anonymous World Services.

Watzlawick, P., J. Beavin, and D. Jackson. *The Pragmatics of Human Com-
    munication.* W. W. Norton, 1967.

Zaleznik, A. "The Dynamics of Subordinacy." In "How Successful Ex-
    ecutives Handle People." *Harvard Business Review*, Studies on
    Communication and Management Skills (1970): 142.

Index

About the Authors

JOHN M. DYCKMAN is a psychotherapist at a large Health Maintenance Organization. He has been a professor of psychology, has conducted research, and has run a private clinical practice for the past 25 years.

JOSEPH A. CUTLER is a psychotherapist at a large Health Maintenance Organization. He has taught university classes in marriage and family counseling and has worked as an Employee Assistance Counselor.